WHAT HAPPENS **AFTER AN** ABORTION?

Also by Jonathan Jeffes:

Abortion: Breaking the Silence in the Church
Unplanned Pregnancy: Talking with Teenagers (Booklet)

WHAT HAPPENS **AFTER AN** ABORTION?

THE OTHER SIDE OF THE STORY

JONATHAN JEFFES

LP LEAN PRESS LIMITED

LP LEAN PRESS LIMITED

First published in Great Britain in 2014 by Lean Press Limited

ISBN: 978-0-9576513-2-6

Lean Press Limited
PO Box 58
26 The Hornet
Chichester
PO19 7BB

Email: info@leanpress.co.uk

Design and typesetting by Andy Ashdown Design
www.andyashdowndesign.co.uk

Cover image: Jaime Monfort

Manufactured in Great Britain by Halcyon

This book is dedicated to:

Sandy Millar and Nicky Gumbel for saving my life through Alpha,
Joanna Thompson for speaking the truth to me,
and David Reardon for getting me started on the way.

Contents

Introduction		9
Chapter 1	How this book came to be written	13
Chapter 2	Overview – understanding why people choose abortion	21
Chapter 3	What happens after an abortion?	31
Chapter 4	A journey through post-abortion healing	49
Chapter 5	Beauty for ashes	63
Chapter 6	Men and abortion	83
Chapter 7	Women and abortion	93
Chapter 8	Shaping an effective personal view	103
Chapter 9	Breaking the silence around abortion	117
Afterword	The importance of breaking the silence	129
Appendix I	Rape and abortion	131
Appendix II	Disability, pre-natal screening and abortion	139
Acknowledgements		146

Introduction

Around 20 years ago I trained to become a crisis pregnancy counsellor. Having become involved in this work in central London, the need to provide counselling for women (and men) who approached us for help with issues pertaining to a past abortion became apparent. Together with Nicky-Sue Leonard I established a post-abortion recovery course, which has been running regularly since 1993. Over the years our counselling team has talked with a wide variety of people of different ages and diverse backgrounds. In total we have counselled over 200 women and around 30 men, most of whom experienced abortion in their early 20s, though some when they were teenagers, and some when they were older.

What follows is based on my experience of running the post-abortion course and contains insights I have found helpful when speaking to others about abortion. The first few chapters outline the story of how I became involved in this work, explain why this book has been written by a man, and outline the separate building blocks that I believe are essential to forming a rounded view of the subject. I address the following questions: What sort of person has an abortion? Why do women become pregnant when they do not want to be? What happens to them afterwards? What differences exist in the way that men and women think about abortion?

Over the years I have often been asked to speak about abortion in small church groups. In these discussion groups someone often says, "Well, it all depends on when you think life begins." The question of when a human life begins frames much of the thinking about abortion in our culture. However, I believe it is completely the wrong question. Perhaps it is more productive to ask, "What happens *after* an abortion? What does the experience of some women and men who maintain a powerful link to a past abortion reveal to us about when life begins?"

This book sets out to answer this question. This approach may appear counter intuitive, but I believe that tackling abortion in this way can make a difficult subject accessible to those who have not previously had an opportunity to engage with it at any substantial level. My hope is that the book will be helpful in building a relevant, compassionate and understanding response to people who are either faced with an unplanned pregnancy, or who have experienced abortion in their past. Although this book has been written primarily for a Christian audience, many of the issues will be of interest to a wider audience.

Over the years, our post-abortion courses have been home to extremely profound conversations as to the nature of abortion and the reasons people ended up in the situations that they did. The book aims to reflect some of the deeper issues that have been raised in our groups – issues that I have rarely heard discussed in public. If the women and men in our groups had a voice, what would they like the reader to know and understand about the connections they made following their abortion? What warnings would they sound? Theirs is the voice of experience. It deserves to be heard.

The last part of the book will explore how individual Christians can build a personal perspective that might help them to avoid abortion in their own lives, as well as ensuring that the culture of our churches responds to the issue with compassion and understanding.

This is the second book I have written on the subject of abortion. The first is *Abortion – Breaking the Silence in the Church*. In the book you are reading I aim to look at what happens after an abortion in greater detail, but two of the chapters – the overview of abortion statistics, and the chapter on developing a personal perspective – have been substantially reproduced in both books, along with selected stories and testimonies.

I have found in general that people are not comfortable thinking about, or discussing, abortion per se, but that they find stories of the women and men we have helped easier to listen to. So, let me begin by telling you one story from our course. I have in my mind a vivid picture of a young woman arriving at one of our first post-abortion groups.

She was in her early 20s and she was wearing a black dress, black top, black boots and a black overcoat. Her face was deathly pale and the skin on her face appeared to be stretched taut, as if to reflect an inner tension. She wore black nail varnish and black lipstick, and her hair was swept back under a black scarf. This was not someone dressed as a 'Goth'; it was a statement. If all the black was striking, what really tore at my heart were her eyes. There was a lifelessness about them – haunted and out of place in one so young. As she entered the room we all stopped talking for a heartbeat. We were used to people arriving on the first evening of our courses looking strained, but this was a dramatic entrance, even by our standards.

Eight weeks later it was the final evening of the course. What a difference! This same woman arrived wearing a flowing white dress. Her lips were bright red and her hair flowed down over her shoulders. She was smiling and her eyes were clear and bright. She was laughing and appeared relaxed and confident.

As she left she thanked us, saying, *"You have restored what was taken by the abortion; I feel [like] a whole woman again"*. About a year later I heard she had married, and a while after that we received a letter telling us she was pregnant. In the letter she thanked us earnestly and said that, had she not been on the course, she did not think she would have married or wanted a child.

Although this woman's appearance was unusual, what was going on under the surface was not. Time after time we saw the same dynamics at work and the same issues surface. There *are* differences in how individuals process their experience, but not as many as one might think given the range of people we have seen. The woman above moved from a life lived in monochrome to one in technicolour. On each course, we prayed that this process of transformation and restoration would be repeated.

My hope for you as a reader – whichever point you are starting from – is that something of this transformation will be available to you in your understanding of the subject of abortion.

Jonathan Jeffes

Chapter 1

How this book came to be written

Over the years, many people have found it unusual for a man to be involved in post-abortion ministry. Women who have come on our courses have also been taken by surprise when they arrived to find a man present. I hesitate to share the story behind my involvement, but a useful point can be made in describing where this journey into post-abortion work began for me.

At the age of 23 I was living in London. I was dating a lovely young Frenchwoman. A few months into our relationship she became unintentionally pregnant. Having discussed the situation, we both thought it best if she had an abortion. My girlfriend did not want to have a child at that point in her life and I did not feel ready to settle down and have children either, so she went ahead with the abortion.

For various reasons, our relationship ended soon after, and I did not see her again for a few years. Then one day a friend, Peter, invited me to go to Paris with him. I remembered that my former girlfriend had since moved back to Paris and I called her when we arrived. Much to my surprise, she answered, and we arranged to meet in a café. The meeting went well and as we talked we were able to resolve some of what had passed between us during the last days of our relationship. We both apologised for our own part of the mess. It was a cathartic experience that removed tension from our shared history. But the story she told me next was one I was not expecting.

My ex-girlfriend was from the south of France and, like all her family, is quite dark in complexion, whereas I have blond hair and blue eyes. She told me that her brother's wife had recently given birth to a son, and that her brother, a true Frenchman and patriot who normally scorned all things English, had insisted on giving his son a very English name – Jonathan: my name. Both her brother and his wife were also dark-featured, but the baby had blond hair and piercing blue eyes. She showed me a photograph. Neither of us said anything, but I could tell that we were both thinking: perhaps this is what our child might have looked like had the baby been born.

Later, after we had said goodbye, a terrible sadness welled up within me and I felt tearful as I walked down the street. This was unusual for me and an acute uneasiness settled over me.

Peter was busy that afternoon, so I decided to visit the Louvre. As I walked around the gallery, I came across an exhibition of seventeenth-century Italian art that was to change my life. One painting really struck me – it depicted the resurrection with Jesus standing outside his tomb. The painting was particularly striking because the artist had depicted Jesus as rather pale and ghost-like, almost as if he were the living dead.

As I looked, I thought to myself, 'You know, that is how Jesus would have appeared to someone looking at him the day after his crucifixion. If you had seen somebody crucified in front of you, and saw them alive again the next day, you would be unable to take it in.' I suddenly thought, 'The guy who painted that picture really believed in this. It wasn't just a story to him.' For the first time in my life the thought came to me, 'What if it really is true? What if this really happened? What if Jesus really did rise from the dead?'

As I stood staring at the painting I immediately *knew*, at a very deep level, that it *was* true and that it really *had* happened: Jesus was the Son of God and he really did physically rise again from the dead. As these thoughts went through my mind, something else began to happen. As I looked at Jesus' figure on the canvas, he came alive. The room in which I was standing seemed to disappear in a blur and suddenly I was somewhere else in the presence of the real, resurrected Jesus, who was alive and standing not two metres in front of me.

I looked at Jesus and Jesus looked at me. You may be thinking, 'How lovely to stand before Jesus, how wonderful it would be to see him in this life.' But it wasn't lovely at all; it was terrifying because there was something wrong with his eyes – they were full of fire, and a terrible piercing flame seemed to come from them. (Later when I read the Bible for the first time I found this verse from Revelation 19:12: "His eyes are like blazing fire.")

At that moment, I understood that Jesus was specifically challenging me about the abortion. Suddenly, the memory of that time came flooding back to my mind. I looked at Jesus and said, "I am so sorry, I did not know." As I said this, everything went back to normal and I was standing in the Louvre in Paris, looking at a painting. I remember thinking, 'I just want to get out of here.' I turned and ran out of the room.

Later, I met Peter and we went for a drink. As we sat there, he said, "What's the matter with you? You look like you've seen a ghost!"

"Something like that," I said, and related the events of the day to him.

On my return to London I found the memory of the incident deeply unsettling. I remained troubled by the powerful effect triggered by the photograph of my ex-girlfriend's nephew.

A few years later a friend invited me to a course in Christian basics called Alpha, and I became a Christian. I began attending a local church, through which I met Joanna Thompson, who was the National Director of CareConfidential, an affiliation of over 130 pregnancy advice centres throughout the UK. We started talking about abortion and I told Joanna about my experience. I said that if I had one clear regret about the past, it was how casually we had made the decision. My girlfriend was a lovely person, and our relationship had been good. Why had we not thought about having the child and giving it a go? Life had not turned out as I had expected afterwards and looking back, I regretted the loss of the relationship and not having the child.

As Joanna told me about her work I became interested in the idea of becoming involved as a counsellor. I wished someone had challenged my thinking all those years ago, and thought that perhaps I could be of use talking with other young men in similar circumstances. A month later CareConfidential ran a conference on how to set up a pregnancy crisis centre. I signed up. Being there with one hundred women felt strange. The few other men who were there were mainly partners of the women attending.

In a seminar entitled 'Post-Abortion Stress and its Effects', the speaker, Sheelagh Clarke, spoke of the strong connection that some women can maintain after their abortions. She went on to list the psychological risks of what she called "post-abortion stress". I listened politely but didn't take it in: what she was saying didn't really make sense to me. I found it hard to believe that women who had gone through an abortion would feel these things.

After the seminar I sat next to Margaret O'Hara at the lunch table. She asked me why I was at the conference. I told her the story of my ex-girlfriend's abortion, my subsequent regrets and my plan to become involved with an advice centre. I mentioned the seminar I had been to, and that I disagreed with what had been said, finding it a bit 'far-fetched'.

At one point in our discussion Margaret said, "I have been thinking about what you told me about your girlfriend's past abortion. A question has come into my mind. If your child had been born, how old would he or she be today?" I immediately replied, "Twelve-and-a-half years old." I can remember the hairs on the back of my neck standing on end. How did I know that? If someone had asked me when my girlfriend had the abortion I would not have been able to answer, not even to within two or three years. I had completely forgotten when it happened, and yet here I was all those years later, knowing exactly to the month how old the child would have been. I found this very disturbing.

At that time, Margaret was running one of the first post-abortion counselling groups. After the conference she took me through a post-abortion counselling course. This came as something of a revelation and turned out to be one of the most difficult, but rewarding, things I have ever done in my life.

During that time I was confronted with some uncomfortable truths that had lain buried deep inside me. At one point I remember feeling a knot in my stomach that seemed to rise up from somewhere deep within me, and a black pall of powerful emotion starting to flood and overwhelm my mind. For a moment I thought something truly awful was happening to me, but it passed as quickly as it had come, leaving me feeling surprisingly calm and peaceful.

Looking back on the experience, it was almost as if the subconscious memories of the missing child had been in my heart all those years, and came out as I processed the thoughts and feelings from the past. I realised that this was something of what I had started to feel talking to my old girlfriend in the café in Paris, especially when she showed me the photograph of her nephew.

As the black and unpleasant moment passed, I suddenly had a clear vision: a vivid picture came into my mind. In my mind's eye I felt as if I was standing at the bottom of a muddy pond. Above on the surface of the water a bright light shone. As I looked up to the shoreline I could see the silhouette of a boy, aged around twelve years old, who stood holding the hand of a tall man. I believe the man was Jesus. I could not quite see the boy clearly but I could see he was looking down at me and smiling. He waved, and then the picture faded and was gone.

As my mind cleared, I felt an extraordinary freedom, as if a great burden had been lifted from my shoulders. This may sound strange, but I believe that I had seen the child I lost through the abortion. I believe that the child is in a place of safety and peace and that, although he is gone, one day we will meet.

As I reached the end of the course, I felt like a completely different person. In hindsight, the abortion had a profound effect on me. This manifested itself in my relationships with women – I hadn't wanted to become close to anyone again and I couldn't even think about having children. A wall of guilt and a feeling of deep, unacknowledged loss had held a part of me prisoner for all those years. Now, many years later I am married and have two children and two stepchildren. I sometimes wonder if this would have happened had I not had the opportunity to meet with Margaret, and subsequently processed my thoughts and feelings.

When I had finished Margaret's counselling, I remembered Sheelagh Clarke's seminar at the conference and her description of the effect that abortion can have. Now it all made much more sense. My personal experience and journey led me to set up the post-abortion counselling group in London. I had found the course to be so life-changing that I wanted to make it available to others, and that is what the superb counselling team headed by Nicky-Sue Leonard, Caryn Dixon, Terese Williamson, Jo Chambers and others have done for many years now.

Earlier, I mentioned that there was a reason why I wanted to tell this story. If someone had told me that one day I would attend a post-abortion counselling course, I would never have believed it. I would have denied that the abortion had a lasting effect on me, and in any case I would never have wanted to go on a counselling course.

Even after I became a Christian, the words of the apostle Paul that we are as 'new creations' (2 Corinthians 5:17) rang true and seemed sufficient. When I became a Christian, I also felt that I had received a direct revelation of forgiveness from the Holy Spirit. But in spite of this, Margaret's question of how old the child would have been was a definite 'trigger' moment.

While I understand that people reading this book may struggle with the idea that abortion can have a profound effect on some people, all I can tell you is that it is true. I say this not because I once had a strange vision, or because I am a Christian now and believe that abortion is wrong. I say this because of my experience of talking with hundreds of people, year after year, for whom this is a very real truth. I have also corresponded with many others, and I am aware of networks of counsellors and organisations throughout the world, all of which are aware of this truth that lies buried beneath the surface in our societies.

I believe that our culture's widespread acceptance of abortion is based on the belief that abortion has no significant undesirable side effects, and that any emotional or psychological toll is less than the emotional or psychological trauma that would be experienced by giving birth following an unintended pregnancy. It is this assumption that I wish to challenge in this book.

Chapter 2

Overview – Understanding why people choose abortion

Have you ever noticed that people *really* dislike talking about abortion? A friend of mine once said, "When the word 'abortion' is mentioned I see people's eyes glaze over." Perhaps the main reason for this is because, like sex and death, many feel it is a private matter that is best not discussed in public. Maybe some people think it does not apply to them – that abortion is something that happens to other people, somewhere else.

However, a startling statistic is that **34% of all women in the United Kingdom will experience at least one abortion in their lifetime.**[1] Or, as a report from The Royal College of Obstetricians and Gynaecologists (*The Care of Women Requesting Induced Abortion*) recognised, "At least one third of women will have had an abortion by the time they reach the age of 45 years."[2]

The truth is that a pandemic of abortion is taking place all around us at every level of our society. It is mostly happening in complete silence and secrecy.

As we will see, unintended pregnancy is no respecter of social class, education level or background in the UK. With the exception of pregnancy and abortion rates for under 18s (where there is a distinct socio-economic geography), unintended pregnancy and abortion occur in every sector of our society. Therefore, it is important that we all engage with and seek to understand abortion because it could well affect us – either personally, or through friends or members of our family.

Who has an abortion?

The majority of women who have abortions are aged between 20 and 25. However, this is the only real differential. Neither social class, income bracket (nor, in some cases, even faith) makes a difference. As revealed in the official Department of Health statistics for abortion in England and Wales,[3] there are minor variations in the demographics, but essentially an unemployed person living in an area of urban deprivation is just as likely to have an abortion as a wealthy, well-educated person living in an affluent area of London.

Although married couples are less likely to choose abortion, 16% of those who had an abortion in 2012 were married.[4] The overwhelming majority (more than 97%) of people choose abortion for 'personal reasons'. Less than 1% of abortions are carried out due to a medical condition affecting the foetus, such as Down's Syndrome.[5] Although rape is a terrible act in our society and official statistics for the number of abortions due to rape are, to my knowledge, not available, it is estimated that the numbers of pregnancies and subsequent abortions due to rape are still mercifully small at less than 1 to 2%. (See Appendix I for further information on the issue of rape and abortion.)

Why do women get pregnant if they do not want to be?

Why do so many women in our society experience an unintended pregnancy and then an abortion? Is it due to ignorance, bad luck or something else?

Studies show that a substantial majority (one authoritative study showed 62%[6], another 86%[7]) of people presenting themselves for an abortion believed that they were using effective contraception. Other findings show that nearly 100% of women having an abortion knew about contraception at the time of conception and probably had access to it. Furthermore, they had almost certainly used some form of contraceptive method in the past.[8]

It is therefore important to understand that, contrary to popular belief, it is not generally a lack of knowledge about contraception that causes an unintended pregnancy resulting in an abortion.

The claim 'Safe sex prevents pregnancy' is often made. However, evidence would seem to suggest otherwise. For example, according to the latest research from the US, if twelve women take oral contraceptives for a year, one will fall pregnant. For condoms the odds are closer to one in six.[9]

Most people in a sexual relationship today believe that with good knowledge of, access to and use of contraception they will not get pregnant and will never 'need' an abortion. In fact, anyone intending to control their fertility using contraception could be at risk of unintended pregnancy due to a complex mix of factors.

If contraception were used in a controlled setting or in a laboratory experiment, some methods would be nearly 100% effective.[10] Of course, the inconvenient truth is that we do not live in a laboratory or in controlled conditions: life gets in the way. In many ways, contraception runs contrary to human nature.

Our experience with the post-abortion recovery course has taught us that the relationship between contraceptive intentions and pregnancy is extremely complex. Over the years, we have heard some seemingly irrational or illogical stories from otherwise highly self-controlled and methodical individuals. The fact of the matter is that human beings are neither entirely rational nor entirely consistent. As CS Lewis put it: "Their [human beings] nearest approach to constancy is undulation – the repeated return to a level from which they repeatedly fall back – a series of troughs and peaks."[11]

Out of our deepest human instinct to be loved and to express love comes, for nearly all of us, the desire to find a partner and have children – to reproduce. This instinct is so powerful that it can drive strong subconscious desires and behaviours. Some women will get pregnant deliberately in an attempt to resolve relationship issues, but many others (sometimes with the encouragement or collusion of the man involved) will become pregnant due to a complex mix of passion, impulse, desire, frustration and circumstances, sometimes with a bit of irrationality or in a moment of madness or abandonment.

From the outside, an observer might describe this behaviour as deliberate or intentional, but men and women who have been in this position are more likely to describe it as an 'accident', or in terms of being overtaken by events or circumstances beyond their control. The increasing use of the phrase "I fell pregnant" seems to reflect a developing, unconscious awareness that we do not control our fertility – that it is something that happens to us regardless of contraceptive choices.

I am not suggesting that women who have abortions get pregnant deliberately, but from what people on our courses tell us, there can be a degree of intentionality – albeit very small – from both women and men with some unintended pregnancies.

I suggest that it is the unrealistic expectation that we can control our own fertility completely that drives the high abortion rate. Contraception may give us partial control over our fertility, but in practice it does not give us absolute control. For nearly half the population, contraception will not prevent pregnancy at least once in their lifetime[12], and one third of our female population will experience at least one abortion. These are the real facts of life.

Why do people choose abortion?

Speaking at the 2008 annual conference of the British Pregnancy Advisory Service (BPAS), CEO Ann Furedi said:

> "We expect to be able to protect ourselves against pregnancy, we expect our birth control to work (though it doesn't always), and we expect to be able to right the wrong when it fails us."[13]

For many of those faced with an unplanned pregnancy we find that – whether men and women will acknowledge this or not – with abortion readily available, this will often seem the easiest, if not the only, choice. For some, the decision is made within a few seconds of the pregnancy being discovered, even for those who never thought they would have an abortion. A woman in a crisis pregnancy has three options: she can give birth and parent the child, she can give birth and release the child for adoption, or she can have an abortion. For all practical purposes a woman in this position – whose expectation of contraception has not been met – may think that abortion is the only realistic choice. Subconsciously, the thought 'if I get pregnant I will have an abortion' may have been in her mind ever since she was a teenager, and this can be a powerful driver towards abortion. Now she is pregnant that thought seems increasingly reasonable.

Women may go through all the stages of welcoming the pregnancy, knowing in their heart of hearts that they will end it. I believe that this is due to the prevailing attitude of society, which has permeated our thinking. It is almost as if society has hijacked our thought processes and we cannot think outside the box. We may not be able to imagine being able to deviate from the norm and actually bring up a child in circumstances that are far from ideal.

Writing in *The Times* in 2007, journalist and mother Caitlin Moran made this frank analysis of her decision to have an abortion when she became unexpectedly pregnant:

> "Last year I had an abortion and I can honestly say it was one of the least difficult decisions of my life. I'm not being flippant when I say it took me longer to decide on what worktops to have in my kitchen than whether I was prepared to spend the rest of my life being responsible for a further human being."[14]

In practice, the option of placing a child for adoption is rarely chosen. Nicky-Sue once asked a pregnant woman whether she had considered adoption as an option instead of abortion. She replied, "If I am going to go through the pregnancy, I will keep the child." It seems that women can often contemplate abortion, but not adoption. Another common response is, "I could never give the child away; only a bad mother would do that." For some today, abortion can be seen as a more compassionate choice than adoption.

For some women, the process of smothering unwelcome thoughts will be easy; for others it will be almost impossible. Many enjoy being pregnant and do all the things they should for a healthy pregnancy, such as giving up smoking, alcohol and unhealthy food. They may also choose to bond with the child. They may work out the due date of the baby and toy with the idea of giving birth. They may go back and forth between deciding to keep the child and deciding to have an abortion, seeking advice from many people, without really making up their minds. They may take folic acid and look at baby clothes in shops at the same time as making an appointment with an abortion clinic. The dilemma experienced is acute and very painful. Many women feel thoroughly overwhelmed by what is happening to them. This is how the women on our course describe their experience of pregnancy leading up to the abortion. It can be a time of great fear and confusion.

The head versus the heart

For some women, it is as if a war literally breaks out inside, a war between the head and the heart. As the pregnancy progresses, the heart begins to call – the instinct to bond with and protect the child can rise up inside a woman and overwhelm her. "Save your child, give life to your baby," the heart pleads. A storm hits, a whirlwind of confusion and doubt driven by the mounting realisation that an abortion will end the life growing within her womb. This realisation can be really frightening. The woman suddenly feels overwhelmed, terrified, boxed in, deserted and alone.

In this crisis of head versus heart, the head has the power – it will make the decision. But the heart fights back with wave after wave of different emotions.

The heart says: "I have always wanted a baby."

The head says: "The time is not right, I will have one when the circumstances allow [be it married, the right house or job, financial situation]."

The heart says: "I love children."

The head says: "I can't give this child the life it should have."

The heart says: "I would never have an abortion."

The head says: "I can't have this child."

Building a wall around her heart, developing tunnel vision

The women on our course often describe how, in order to make the decision for an abortion, they had to build a wall around their hearts, blocking off their maternal instincts and the excitement about having the child. Only then could they bear to take the necessary steps to go through with the abortion.

As the time for the abortion approaches, the women and men we have spoken with describe developing tunnel vision, focusing on abortion as the solution. They consciously block out unwelcome feelings and doubts so that abortion becomes the obvious choice. It appears to offer a way out: the ability to get off the 'roller coaster' and for life to return to the same place it was before the discovery of the pregnancy.

Above all, abortion appears to offer the tantalising possibility that, within a few days or weeks, the difficult situation will be forgotten and life will return to normal. As people smother their doubts, the abortion clinic may be seen as a place of refuge from the storm and an island of peace that offers them protection: a place of non-judgment, sympathy and understanding.

My heart has gone out to every person I have met during a crisis pregnancy. At a time when their world has been turned upside down, the abortion offers to wind back the clock and return them to where they were before the pregnancy. The perceived promise is that with a simple procedure the turmoil will stop and life will be back to normal. Having spoken to many people in this situation it can be tempting to agree that abortion might well be the best course of action in their seemingly hopeless predicament. However, our experience on the post-abortion course has shown us that often they are simply exchanging one set of problems for another.

Chapter 3

What happens after an abortion?

In the last chapter we saw how people choosing abortion tend to develop 'tunnel vision' to smother unwelcome thoughts and feelings. Their hope is that the turmoil will stop and be forgotten soon after the abortion. However, for some people, life after an abortion can turn out to be more complicated than they expected. At the heart of the issue lies the memory of the pregnancy. Abortion is chosen because the pregnancy is not wanted. But after a termination, the fact (and memory) of the pregnancy has the potential to maintain a powerful and unwelcome link to the past that cannot easily be broken. For some, unwelcome thoughts and feelings that can have a profound effect on their lives begin to surface unexpectedly.

To illustrate what might happen next, I have constructed a 'blended' narrative. This is a fictionalised account designed to reflect the thoughts and feelings that a woman might experience in the weeks and months after an abortion. The narrative is based on real events, thoughts and feelings that individuals have related to me during our courses. Presenting it as a 'blended' account allows me to remove the more subjective or personal aspects of what can emerge from one individual experience and, I believe, presents a more average and realistic picture of what has been related to us over the years in our groups.

Although men can also be deeply affected by an abortion, the next three chapters will focus mainly on the experience of women. Chapter 6 focuses specifically on men.

In spite of what Tom (my boyfriend at the time) said, I never wanted to get pregnant and never imagined I would need an abortion. We talked about having the baby a little bit, but neither of us wanted the commitment; it just didn't seem possible. At the clinic the counsellor said there was an appointment available the following week, so I went ahead and booked it. Not wanting to think too much, I put the appointment out of my mind as much as possible. There was a moment at the door of the clinic when, just for a second, a moment of doubt crept in and I wondered if I was doing the right thing. But I put these doubts out of my mind, gritted my teeth and went ahead with the abortion.

When I came out of the clinic afterwards the sun was shining. I felt a surge of elation and excitement. Tension had been high since the discovery of the pregnancy and now it was all over, life could get back to normal! I was off the hook. Tom met me in the clinic's car park and took me home. He looked happy and relieved, but there was an uncomfortable silence between us at times in the car. He seemed unable to look me in the eye.

When we arrived home I felt tired. "It's only natural, you have been through a lot," Tom said. My mood began to change. The relief I had felt immediately after the abortion gave way to something else. For a while

I felt sad and tearful; I didn't want to think why this was. Tom left for work and I went into the bedroom and lay down to sleep. As I lay there my mind drifted back to the events of the past few weeks. Suddenly a dark and frightening emotion started to well up inside. Memories of the crisis began to come back –thoughts of what it would be like to be a mother and to have the child, and I remembered what it was like to be pregnant.

As these memories surfaced, what I can only describe as a dark cloud descended on my mind. It was like a suffocating blackness. At some level in my subconscious there was a connection that I had not wanted to make before the abortion. It began to surface in my mind now. It was something awful, too dreadful to face. I tried to push it out of my mind, to stifle the connection, but I began to experience some of the emotions from the crisis again, wildly swinging from the excitement at being pregnant to the terror of the thought of giving birth and being responsible for another human being. I started to sweat and shudder.

I ran into the bathroom and threw up. Tears came, followed by a crashing headache. The clinic had warned that I might feel a bit low for a couple of days as my hormones readjusted. "Maybe that's what's happening," I told myself. I had been given some painkillers and was told to come back if there were any problems. I decided I would give it a couple of days and see if I felt any better.

As I looked at myself in the bathroom mirror the unfamiliar emotions overwhelmed my mind. I steadied myself against the sink and looked at my reflection. "Pull yourself together," I said aloud. Taking a deep breath and looking into my reflection I announced to the bathroom, "I am going to get on with life, and I am not going to think about this any more. In fact, I am never going to think about this ever again."

I remember consciously pushing the whole disaster out of my mind – the experience of the abortion, what it was like to be pregnant, my feelings before and my feelings at that moment. I wanted to bury the memories, never to think about it again. As I did this, calmness returned. I went back into the bedroom, lay down and fell asleep. The next morning I felt better, if a little numb. "It's only natural," I said to myself, "Your body is getting back to normal."

Life did return to normal to a certain extent, but the feeling of numbness persisted. Tom seemed increasingly uncomfortable in my presence, and one evening, following an argument in which he blamed me for getting pregnant, we agreed that it would be best if we stopped seeing each other. So, I returned to what I knew – working hard and enjoying life.

For a while, life went back to how it had been before the abortion, except that something had changed. The activities I used to enjoy – eating out, seeing films and spending time with my friends – didn't seem to bring the same level of enjoyment as before. I felt flat. One day I was watching a film. I began to feel uncomfortable as a scene depicted a mother giving birth. I felt a strong sense of anger towards the man in the film, and afterwards I drank a little too much wine to help me get over the intrusive emotion.

One day, some months later, I suddenly became upset and depressed. I told myself I didn't know why, but deep down I did know: it was the day the child would have been born. That night I cried myself to sleep.

Life moved on and I started to work very hard, staying late at the office most evenings. I felt I needed some space after my split with Tom and did not want another boyfriend at that point. I noticed myself avoiding men who approached me, wanting to keep them at arm's length. Occasionally I did have sex, but only for one night because I did not want emotional complications. Cathy, my best friend, noticed the change and asked me if everything was all right. She was the only person who knew about the abortion, but she never asked me about it specifically.

Before the abortion, I had a strong Christian faith, but since the discovery of the pregnancy I found it difficult to pray and had stopped going to church. After the abortion I avoided my Christian friends.

One day on the bus, I noticed a small child looking at me intently and felt uncomfortable. I started to notice a creeping feeling of loneliness and isolation that came over me when I was with others, perhaps at a party or with my female friends. As a couple of years went by I was painfully aware of the anniversary date of both the abortion and when the child would have been born. These dates troubled me as they came round. Sometimes when I woke in the morning, thoughts of the abortion procedure would come to my mind. Sometimes I would experience vivid dreams of a child – a small boy. Once I dreamt of a child standing alone on a beach, looking for his mother.

Who is most likely to be impacted by a past abortion?

After an abortion people seem to be divided into one of two groups: those who are seemingly unaffected by their experience and those who are – to a greater or lesser degree – affected by it. I believe that the degree to which someone will be impacted by an abortion is influenced by a complex mix of personality, life experience, the circumstances surrounding the pregnancy and abortion, and the degree to which someone makes their life work afterwards. For some, but not all, the after-effects seem to be influenced by pre-existing mental health or behavioural issues that perhaps contributed to the abortion decision in the first place.

However, my personal view is that it would be a mistake to view emotional complications after an abortion as something that only happens to those with a latent or pre-existing behavioural or mental health problem. It seems to me that sometimes the strongest, most confident and highly educated people can be just as affected as those with a history of dysfunctional relationships or depression that pre-dated their abortion.

Indeed, it might be possible to argue the opposite for some. On the course, we noted that women and men, for whom an abortion was their first setback in life or their first serious encounter with an emotional trauma or problem, were particularly vulnerable to after-effects. It seemed that this group lacked the coping strategies that others with pre-existing problems might have developed before their abortions, and which might have helped them afterwards. For example, one woman who had had an unhappy childhood was used to expressing strong emotions and, as a result, had been able to do a lot of crying and grieving before coming on the course. Other factors that seemed to leave individuals vulnerable to strong after-effects were situations in which a high degree of pressure had been applied by others, (for example by parents or partners), or where the abortion went against strongly held religious, moral or cultural beliefs.

So, while it is fair to say that sometimes an abortion can sit on top of other behavioural or emotional problems, which perhaps contributed to the pregnancy and subsequent abortion, this is not always the case. The majority of women on our courses have not had complex histories of mental health issues, but the abortion still deeply impacted them. The fact that women from all walks of life seek help through post-abortion recovery programmes such as ours, and are able to deal with their difficulties within the context of the group, suggest that their abortions were the direct cause of these difficulties. This is what those on our courses have told us.

For many, an abortion can act as an impetus to make their lives work better afterwards. Perhaps this group views it as a narrow escape and the abortion can be seen in positive terms, allowing their new, 'redeemed' life to come into being: a new start, as it were. For those who are able to move on and rebuild a successful life, perhaps including success at work or with a partner or family, the abortion may appear to recede into the past and be forgotten.

However, even for this group, events later in life or unexpected emotions may subsequently (sometimes suddenly) trigger a powerful connection with the abortion experience, often many years after the event.

The conclusions about the after-effects of abortion in this book are based on discussions within our courses, and I make no claim outside of this. Although we believe that the experience represented here may well be widespread, we know it is not universal and many women and men go through abortion seemingly untouched. My purpose here is not to highlight the number of women and men who may have been impacted by abortion, but to explore its effects from the perspective of someone who *has* made a subsequent connection with their experience. I believe that this perspective can lead to a deeper understanding of the subject.

What happens afterwards?

As we read in the blended narrative, immediately after an abortion, many women feel enormous relief and immerse themselves in their lives again, trusting that everything will go back to normal. They cling to the belief that the abortion was just a medical procedure and was the best option for everyone concerned. They may heavily invest their energy in areas connected with the reasons why they could not have the child, such as: schoolwork, relationships with partners, social lives, studies at university, career or family.

Others know immediately that they have done something that is going to cause them pain. They experience a feeling of emptiness inside, as well as regret for the loss of their child. They may feel they have done something wrong – perhaps even something unforgivable. As a woman's hormones readjust she may experience mood swings and unpleasant memories of the day the abortion took place.

In the face of this, women try to push the whole experience to the back of their minds. It is as if they take a big metal storage box and put everything to do with the abortion into it: the fears and agonies in making the decision, the memories of the abortion itself, any desires for a child, and thoughts about the child they have lost and who he or she might have been. Then they push the box into the darkest corner of their mind, put a large padlock on it, and carry on, pretending that it doesn't exist.

However, sooner or later they may find that this is not the end of the story. Something has changed: something physical, emotional and spiritual. This may manifest itself in a feeling of sadness or a creeping guilt. They may feel alone and distant from others and may feel depressed, emotionally numb, worthless, and perhaps angry with those who contributed to the abortion decision.

Some may respond to these feelings by keeping busy and pouring their energy into life. But, over time, some women find their efforts are in vain. Painful feelings and memories and a determination not to acknowledge the lost child as a child have been put into the box. Equally, women may have put good things in the box, such as: creativity, the desire to be a parent, vulnerability, self-respect or their tenderness as a lover, meaning that they remain cut off from these positive things. If we return to the image of the wall that a woman can build around her heart before the abortion, there can be so much of herself locked in behind that wall that her emotions, both good and bad, can become a jumble. The emotions are impossible to deal with, yet endlessly felt.

For women in this situation, the sense of loss and self-blame may gradually increase as the pressure builds from within. A woman may stop liking herself, believing that she is a bad person. She may seek to quench these negative feelings in a variety of ways: striving to be successful or to be a perfect mother to her other children. She may focus on keeping busy, perhaps using alcohol to numb the pain; or she may live recklessly, for example through a promiscuous lifestyle. These behaviours can all be an attempt to hide from the thoughts and emotions leaking out of the big metal storage box hidden in the corner.

Due to the role they played in deciding to have an abortion, some women may feel that they deserve punishment and either inflict it on themselves, or receive it from others. For example, they may enter into destructive relationships, begin self-harming or develop anorexia. If they have acknowledged the child as a child, they may not feel that they have the right to grieve their loss, which may cause a lingering, unresolved sorrow. The most common comment we hear is: "a part of me died that day". There is a persistent feeling that something fundamental has been taken away by the abortion.

I appreciate that the idea that people can be seriously impacted by an abortion may be difficult to understand at first, or perhaps dismissed by the thought that whatever is experienced must be better than bringing an 'unwanted' child into the world. Before an abortion there can be a strong desire to perceive abortion in terms of gain – gaining freedom, gaining control over life and reproduction. What is not widely understood is the degree of loss that can be experienced, and the sheer scale of what can be taken away by an abortion.

Perhaps a good place to begin to understand the effects of an abortion is to list some of the comments that we have heard from the guests on our courses. One of the exercises that we do on the course is to list answers to two questions on a flip chart. First, "What have I lost through the abortion?" and second, "How has my abortion affected me?" The following are actual replies to these questions from one recent course attended by eight women:

1. What have I lost through the abortion?

   Confidence
   Ability to enjoy myself
   Self-worth
   Womanhood
   Closeness with God
   Motherhood
   Ability to connect to people/things around me
   A child

2. How has my abortion affected me?

   Loss of identity
   Difficulty in relating
   Preoccupation with dying
   Wanting to die

Suicidal thoughts
Self-destruction
Serious thoughts about life, society and my place
Preoccupation about childhood
A part of me has died
Deserve bad things and no happiness
Loss of weight/nausea/sickness
Anxiety
Deserve punishment
Nervous before periods
Loss of inner peace
Loss of relationship with God

These are the comments from one exercise from *one* course. The important point to make from these lists is that for most of the women on our courses, the sheer scale of the loss invalidated their original decision, which had been mainly perceived and evaluated in terms of gain.

We have seen people put a wide range of these and other issues behind them as they process and resolve their past abortion through the course. Such problems can include, among others: eating disorders, sleep problems, feelings of unworthiness, self-punishment, low self-esteem and alcohol or drug misuse. Listed below are the most common issues that we have experienced in our groups: factors that can sap a person's energy and result in a corrosive effect on their morale and relationships.

A fear of intimacy or commitment

It is striking among those we counsel that there can be a fear of intimacy or commitment in relationships. Perhaps people wish to stay away from emotions that remind them of the pregnancy, and the emotional steps along the way that resulted in the abortion. This can lead people into only wanting temporary relationships or embracing a promiscuous lifestyle, or choosing not to enter into any romantic relationship at all.

Isolation

A woman who has experienced an abortion can feel very alone. It is as if a veil of silence and secrecy descends. Although some people may talk about abortion as an 'issue', few want to hear that someone has had an abortion or how it may have affected her. There is no public acknowledgement of the existence of the child, so there is no obvious compassion for her loss.

A partner may expect a woman to bounce back as quickly as she might after a minor operation, giving no thought to what has actually taken place. The woman may want to distance herself from others, thinking, 'Nobody understands how I feel.' A strong desire for secrecy – the idea that 'no one must know' – further compounds her sense of isolation and loneliness.

Fear of having children

Those who have been through abortion may be worried about having children in the future. For some, even the sight of children or pregnant women may be upsetting, and they may keep their distance from friends or relatives who have children. They may feel they do not deserve to have a family in the future, or develop a tendency to overprotect children when they do arrive. Women can also be secretly worried that the abortion may have damaged their reproductive ability.

Loss of confidence in others

We might like to think of our society with its government institutions and infrastructure as a caring society: for example, we care about the homeless and animal welfare. We expect society to care about families and the wellbeing of those around us. The feelings of loss and depression that can surface after an abortion can make people question that society cares about them. It can leave people feeling that abortion was brutal and uncaring: they feel that a terrible act has been done to them by the medical profession, and by the society that permits it.

We will see in a later chapter that women can also feel forced into a corner and exploited by men. The subsequent feeling of emptiness can have a corrosive effect on their confidence, and on their relationships with the opposite sex, as well as causing uncertainty about their position and role in life.

Potential relationship breakdown

Many of those who have come on our courses have suffered relationship breakdown following an abortion. The abortion decision can underline an existing lack of commitment or weaknesses in a relationship, and the subsequent guilt can drive people apart. An abortion experience can introduce tension into a relationship or marriage if one partner wanted it more than the other. Creating something together – a new life – and then deciding to go ahead with an abortion, often leads to tension. At the time of the decision a woman might feel forced to choose between the relationship and the unborn child. In many cases she loses both. If the relationship continues, sex can become a problem with a strong desire to avoid another pregnancy on the part of the woman.

Risk of repeat abortions

Abortion seems to leave people at risk of further abortions: one third of all abortions are repeat procedures.[15] Paradoxically, there is a known tendency for some women to repeat the experience, either to reassure themselves that they are still fertile, or out of a desire to be pregnant again at a time of their own choosing. The term 'atonement child' refers to a situation where a woman deliberately conceives a child following an abortion, driven by feelings of guilt and remorse. Other factors leaving an individual at risk of repeat abortions may include dysfunction in relationships and low self-esteem.

Depression

If not addressed, the emotions that lie buried in the 'storage box' mentioned above can become a corrosive source of lingering sadness and bitterness, sapping energy and leading to depression.

What about those who are apparently unaffected?

Some women and men may think of, and/or talk about, their abortions as 'no big deal'. But, as we have already indicated, even those who are apparently unaffected by an abortion may subsequently, sometimes many years later, experience dramatic 'trigger points': events that suddenly make a connection with the past abortion.

My story, which I related at the beginning of this book, is one example of just such a trigger. Being asked how old the child would have been and knowing the age to within a few months came as a shock to me.

In our groups, one woman felt overwhelmed when a later child was born. Pictures of foetal development in a magazine shocked another. One woman met up with a friend whose child had been born around the time of her abortion and the sight of the child suddenly connected her with her lost pregnancy. The most common trigger is becoming pregnant and giving birth to a subsequent, 'wanted' child.

Life changes, such at the onset of menopause, can also act as a trigger mechanism for a woman. Emotions stemming from these events can be unexpectedly powerful when they do appear, because they have not been processed or resolved. They can thus be experienced as if the abortion had happened just yesterday.

It is our belief that anyone who experiences an abortion has the potential to make this subsequent connection. There is a saying that 'time heals'. From what we have seen from the men and women on our courses, time can be a part of healing, but on its own it is not a source of healing. The emotional effects of an abortion can surface powerfully many years after the event. We do not know why some do not make a subsequent connection; we run the course for those who do, so by definition we only deal with people who have already made this connection.

What causes the effects?

I believe that the instinct to create and nurture life is one of our deepest and most profound human desires. For many women, few experiences can compare to the wonder felt when a pregnancy is discovered, especially for the first time. Pregnancy bestows a mantle of parenthood upon a woman, and also upon a man.

At the moment a woman discovers she is pregnant she finds herself as a mother. A man finds himself as a father. A new life has begun. With the onset of pregnancy a woman's body and mind begin to prepare for the arrival of her child. Her maternal instincts may begin to come into play, even if she is already planning to end the pregnancy with an abortion. The truth is that without an abortion a child would have been born. Five or six months later a birth would have taken place.

The fact is that abortion is not a time machine: it does not turn back the clock, or take a woman back to where she was *before* she became pregnant. It does not make a woman as if she had never been pregnant. She will always be a woman who has experienced a pregnancy.

At a very deep level, pregnancy – no matter how brief – connects men and women with their child. Abortion leaves them suspended or disconnected. People may not like to think that a child is growing in the womb before an abortion, but afterwards the memory of the pregnancy and the bond that was established at its discovery can maintain a powerful connection with the lost child.

It is common to begin to feel strong emotions of loss and guilt, sometimes lying buried and unacknowledged, which produce the effects described above. We believe that these effects can be felt even if a conscious connection has not been made. If a connection *is* made and subsequently not addressed, these effects have the potential to start overwhelming an individual and to seriously impact his or her life.

There is one particular issue that has the potential to be extremely destructive. Over many years we have seen nearly everyone discover this same surprising issue, sometimes lying hidden beneath the others. When it comes, the moment of discovery can be sudden and dramatic. It can be a troubling and painful connection to make, but ultimately it is the gateway to healing and reconciliation, and understanding it is the key to recovery. To help us understand the full significance of this moment I would like to reveal it in the way that we approach it on the post-abortion recovery course. I would like to take us on the same journey that we have taken so many times over the last 20 years.

Chapter 4

A journey through post-abortion healing

Recovery after an abortion: to get over it, you have to go through it

In a recent newspaper article, international rugby player Brian Moore spoke movingly about how the experience of suppressing memories of childhood abuse had affected him: "The problem is, if you don't let yourself feel it, you don't get through it. You can't say you don't think about it, because you don't know where it is surfacing."[16] His comment reminded me of the many stories we have heard on our post-abortion counselling course of what happens when people bottle up and suppress memories and emotions instead of processing and working through them.

It may take a lot of courage for a woman or a man to admit to themselves that the difficulties they are experiencing may be due to the unexpected consequences of abortion. The prospect of exploring painful events and memories from the past can be daunting, but the time may come when they feel they should be addressed. This is when we hope that they will seek out help, such as a post-abortion recovery group, or one-to-one counselling.

Our course follows a carefully structured programme, which is designed to help women and men work through the issues in their own way, in their own time, and with the help and support they need to deal with the problems and emotions that are raised.

We work hard to create a welcoming, confidential environment – a place of safety where people are free to explore their own experiences and feelings and their inmost fears and worries. Over the years of running the course, our leaders and helpers have worked with a broad spectrum of people with widely differing experiences. As a result they have developed a real insight and understanding of the issues raised. Post-abortion courses can be offered in a one-to-one counselling situation. However, our team concentrated on running groups. This worked well for us, as the group can learn from each other's experiences and support each other through the various stages.

At the start of the course, there may be a sense of heaviness, of carrying a burden. People sometimes use the word 'stuck' and say they are emotionally exhausted. One woman described herself as a balloon about to go pop: she feared her inner tension. Perhaps for most, the hardest step is what takes place on the first evening – the moment that they take off the padlock and prise open the lid of the storage box that they have pushed into the furthest corner of their mind.

When the lid is opened, the first emotion to be expressed in the group is often one of anger. Sometimes a barely controlled rage bursts out during the group discussion on that first evening. The anger is directed mainly at the man involved in the pregnancy, but it can also be directed at the woman herself, or perhaps towards society and the process for obtaining an abortion.

The anger can be a self-protection mechanism designed to shield an individual from other emotions or memories. Once expressed, the anger usually seems to dissipate. Then another emotion makes itself felt: a deep sense of guilt and shame. For some, their abortions went against their core values and beliefs and they can develop a strong feeling of guilt afterwards. Even if a woman or man had no sense beforehand that abortion was wrong, afterwards there may well be an unexpected feeling of having done something wrong. This sense of guilt and shame can become the source of feelings of isolation and loneliness, as described in the previous chapter.

An awareness of shame can help people begin to process their thoughts and feelings, and enable them to identify some of the issues that they need to resolve. This can ease some of the inner tension and bring clarity of thought. One woman said it was like joining up the numbered dots of a picture puzzle. At first it did not make sense, but as she joined the dots a clear image began to emerge.

It can be very difficult to help people through the next stage. We do not tell people what to think and we do not push them into feeling or thinking anything. We let each person make their own connections, in their own time, at whatever level is useful to them. But as they do this, they may start to identify an overpowering feeling of loss and struggle to identify its cause. Initially they may have general feelings of loss associated with the abortion – perhaps loss of innocence or self-esteem. They may mourn the loss of a relationship if it ended after the abortion. What they are not prepared for are the deeper feelings of grief and sorrow that can begin to emerge as they make a direct connection with the child that was lost through the abortion.

To illustrate what happens next I have written another 'blended' account. It is in two parts, the first part outlining what happens when this connection is made, and the second part showing the stages that bring release and healing. Again, all of these thoughts and emotions are based on real experiences of people who have taken our courses.

On the first evening of the post-abortion course I really didn't want to go, sensing that something unpleasant might happen. My friend Hanna had done the course a year ago and she seemed like a different person afterwards. She had told me her story one night and I confided in her, telling the story of my own abortion. She persuaded me to sign up. As I went to the first session I became aware of a desire for secrecy – I didn't want anyone to see me travelling to the venue. The strength of this feeling made me realise how much I had been covering it all up, and I thought what a relief it would be to deal with it – to get it out in the open.

As I arrived at the room where the course was being held, I was reassured by the friendly welcome and the wide range of 'normal' looking people. Perhaps it would not be so bad after all. On that first evening, the leader encouraged some in the group to tell their stories and to think about how we all felt. I was surprised by some of the stories, which closely mirrored my own experience, and also at how interesting the evening had been. There were serious moments, but also lots of laughter.

As the course progressed over the next three weeks, I became aware of strong emotions that I had not wanted to acknowledge, especially a sense of anger, directed towards my ex-boyfriend, Tom, and also of disappointment with myself. I had always had a strong motherly instinct and I knew that I wanted to be a mother one day. So, how could I have gone through with the abortion? As I thought about the past and what I was feeling and experiencing now, I could begin to see that I had been harbouring a strong feeling of shame, which had been holding part of me prisoner all that time.

Once these emotions had been identified and discussed, their power lessened and became dim. But this process was like peeling away the layers of an onion, and something else then made itself felt. I tried to avoid it at first, but then it became quite clear. It was the part I did not want to think about, the thing that had been locked away inside me. The thing I promised myself, as I stared into the bathroom mirror that day after the abortion, that I would never, ever have to think about.

But now I was ready to face it. I dropped my guard and let it come. A picture came into my mind, breath-taking in its clarity. As it came into focus I knew exactly what it was, and it broke my heart. I could see my child – the baby lost through the abortion.

At first I could not believe how vivid his image was in my mind. He was three years old, with curly hair and clear, beautiful eyes. He was strong, and in my mind's eye he reached out for me with a lovely, perfect little hand. I gasped and felt short of breath; the room started to spin. I knew his name. I cried out for him and started to weep. I shook and for a few minutes feared I was losing control. Wave after wave of sorrow, sadness and remorse flooded over me.

There is one central issue that has the potential to confront anyone who has experienced an abortion. This issue is, to a great extent, what drives the effects we read about in the previous chapter. It is *the reality of the child that was lost.*

Some will have a clear sense of whether their child was a boy or a girl. Some, out of an unconscious longing, may have named their child. They may have an idea of the colour of his or her eyes and hair. They may experience intense dreams of the child. Some will know exactly to the day when that child would have been born and every year they will remember the due date, and be aware of the child's exact age. For some, the images of the child grow in their minds as the years pass, so they can see how they would have looked as they grew older.

On our course, the opportunity is given to women and men to express their feelings through letters, poems or artwork. The work they create can be intense in its longing and sensuousness: they portray vivid images of the lost children, their longing to hold and nurture them, to see them grow, to take their first steps and to gaze into their eyes. The yearning is powerful and real.

Those who have never given thought to what happens after an abortion may think that this is a bit over the top – a bit sentimental or mawkish. After all, abortion is legal. The woman has done nothing wrong; she has nothing to be ashamed of. Some think that this was her choice so she should live with it and move on.

Some who may not have made a connection with their own past abortion may even think that a course such as ours might encourage harmful self-indulgence or an unhelpful attachment to the child and that people should simply 'get over it'. But, let us consider the loss of miscarriage. Those who have experienced this will know that it can be felt as a searing pain, and every bit as keenly as the loss of a baby carried to full term. The loss can be felt years after the event as the lost child continues to be mourned and remembered.

The connection after an abortion has the potential to be as powerful as that of a miscarriage, or even a born child. Those who make this connection can find themselves in a place of grief and darkness. On our courses we have witnessed the depths of grief expressed as women weep for their lost children. I have also witnessed men crying as they made a similar connection.

For both men and women, there can be an almost overwhelming sense of loss and sorrow. But they are then also confronted with another reality: the part they personally played in deciding to end the pregnancy. For some, the growing realisation that they have participated in denying their child the opportunity of life can leave them in a place of pain, feeling that they have done something terrible, and even unforgivable.

A painful time can follow as they make these connections, but they will then move on through a process that acknowledges the loss and helps to bring healing and restoration.

The next week was difficult. I experienced terrible moments of sadness and remorse, and at night I wept for my lost baby. But after some time the feeling of sadness started to lift and I felt calm. In the session the following week I realised that the other women had been going through a similar experience as they grieved for their lost children.

Then came the next stage, the one that I would not have had the courage to face before. As I reflected upon the decision to have the abortion I realised that I had been carrying the thought that I was responsible for ending the life of my own child. As I thought about this, guilt and shame rose up. It was almost too painful to deal with.

Strangely, as I faced the responsibility for what had happened, it no longer seemed as daunting now that the feelings of sorrow and grief had started to clear and diminish. The feelings had been a barrier – a wall that prevented me from thinking about the abortion and the past. But now that there was less to fear, I felt that I could face my responsibility for what had happened. As I did so, I felt a burden lifting from my shoulders.

I was no longer angry at Tom and the adviser at the abortion clinic.

As I forgave Tom I started to feel a peace I had not known for a long time. I was also able to begin the process of forgiving myself, although I felt this would take some time. As the crushing feeling of shame started to lift I began to feel a fresh optimism about the future. I also started to reconnect with my faith and managed to pray to God that he would forgive my abortion.

The course leaders invited anyone who wished to share in Communion, as a ceremony of repentance and reconciliation. It was a powerful time. In the moments after this simple act the last piece of the jigsaw fell into place.

I managed to do the hardest thing of all: to surrender my lost child to God for safekeeping until a time comes when I know we will be reunited in the afterlife. I spoke out his name, the name that came into my mind when I first saw the picture of my baby in my mind's eye. I claimed this name aloud for my child and, in my heart, let him go into the protective arms of Jesus. He will look after him, he will protect him and he will keep him in a place of safety and peace.

During the following week I found myself going past a garden centre. I went in and bought a small rosebush. I planted it in my garden in memory of the child that was lost. I did not find this painful, but reassuring and life affirming, as if I was reclaiming a part of my life. I realised that together with the negative feelings I did not want to think about, I had also shut away many good things: my desire to have a family, to be emotionally vulnerable with a man, feelings of tenderness and even my self-respect.

Two weeks later, at the end of the course, I could not believe what had happened to me. It was like coming back to life from a dead place. I felt whole again and ready to face the future. Now that the heaviness had gone I became aware of the extent to which I had built a wall around myself and cut myself off from others. Although I still felt sad about losing the child, the memories and thoughts were no longer intrusive. They no longer had a hold over me. I felt joy and new life. I was free.

Healing, forgiveness and restoration

At the start of the course, people expect that they will struggle with issues of accountability and forgiveness – especially forgiving someone else. They are often unprepared for the rawness and power of their feelings of grief as they face up to the loss of their child. These feelings can be particularly strong for women who really wanted to keep their child, for those who had their abortions recently, and for those who feel that the abortion has created a separation between them and God. However, identifying the feelings can be the start of the healing process, and as they engage with them, their power lessens. This may take a few days, or for some a while longer, but as the feelings of grief begin to lift people find the sense of inner tension that led them to the course has eased. Life starts to return to normal. Once the burden has been lifted from the heart, the head can once again think clearly about the past. So, by the time we get to the stage of considering accountability and forgiveness, these issues seem less difficult than they may have appeared at first.

Forgiveness is not a magic trick; it is not like a rabbit that one can take out of a hat and wave around, put back in the hat and then move on. It is a process that needs to be truthfully and sincerely worked through. For a woman or man to receive forgiveness and to forgive others, they have to examine honestly the circumstances leading to the abortion, resolving as best they can those things for which they, and those things for which others, are responsible.

The most common question we are asked by Christians who have had an abortion, or whose partners have had an abortion, is, "Why is it that I pray for forgiveness and yet don't *feel* forgiven?" For Christians to come to a place of receiving forgiveness it is necessary to engage with what has taken place. It is hard to pray sincerely for forgiveness while at the same time thinking, "I am glad that it happened," or even, "I am glad the abortion took place before I became a Christian."

The key to freedom is forgiveness, and the key to forgiveness is effective repentance. A helpful working definition of repentance is this: "Rewind the video. If you were back in the same situation now, with your current understanding and experience, would you try to do things differently?"

I do understand that for some, the abortion decision was made as a result of extremely traumatic circumstances, and saying that they would have done something different might not reflect a likely situation. However, we found that it is helpful for both women and men if they can come to a point where they can honestly say: "If I were back there, as the person I am now, I would fight to keep the child. I would do things differently, including thinking about the option of adoption if necessary." This does not mean being pre-occupied with the past, or having unrealistic expectations about what they would or would not have done, but it does mean thinking the process through and at least having a *desire* to have chosen differently. This can be very complicated to do on one's own, which is where a course like ours can help.

For Christians, healing, forgiveness and restoration can take place within the context of their faith. For those of no faith, or of a different faith, working through the issues and resolving them still brings healing and peace. There are various organisations and counsellors around the country who offer post-abortion counselling both in groups and on a one-to-one basis. It is not necessary for participants to be Christians, and I would encourage anyone who is struggling with a past abortion to seek out a course or counsellor in their local area.

For those who do make a connection with a past abortion, we believe God is eager to reach out to women and men who have been through abortion. He is a God of compassion and he knows that there is a second victim of abortion: the mother (and thirdly the father).

God seeks to reach out to women and men by his grace, to heal and restore them and to help them to face the issues from a past abortion within the shadow of his cross, where healing and new life are poured out. Abortion is not the unforgivable sin; God can and will bring healing as people have the courage to come to him with their storage boxes and explore the contents with him.

Below are some comments, insights and thoughts from women reflecting on their experiences at recent courses. These comments were recorded in the feedback questionnaires at the end of the course:

Abortion is profoundly damaging. It is not just a baby's life that is destroyed; it is also the mother's life. Far from preventing mental distress (the grounds on which abortion is technically approved), it is the direct cause of it. The grief of losing a child is something that cannot be qualified or imagined until it happens, and often it is many years down the line from the original event.

A, aged 34

I had felt numb for a very long time about the abortion and then when my sister became pregnant I realised I needed to deal with some "stuff". I became aware of issues I hadn't faced, and a feeling of guilt over not protecting, or even having that instinct to protect, my baby. I heard good things about your course from a friend and booked myself on.

I keep thinking of the word "reconnected" and I think I got reconnected to my feelings [on the course]. I now feel a sense of loss that I didn't understand before; I had the loss but not the words or the structure to see that actually I was grieving the loss of my child. The course has helped me unravel, or at least start to unravel, what has been going on. I've met some wonderfully brave women and been treated with such care. It's been really helpful to hear other people's stories and realise I am not alone in my reactions.

C, aged 28

Abortion is not one "act". It is a series of complicated and intricate acts that shape you.

S, aged 32

One woman who had five abortions wrote: *"I would never encourage anyone to do it. I would also let them know that as much as the doctors and medical profession would see it as minor, it is a major thing emotionally and spiritually."*

N, aged 29

Abortion is never an easy choice and ultimately it destroys both a woman and her unborn child. There is always a way that a problem can be worked through!

M, aged 41

Don't do it! If you think you are strong, you are not; this tears you apart. Don't believe everything your doctor tells you. You can fall pregnant regardless!

C, aged 23

I would say don't have an abortion, because it really messes you up, especially if you involve family and friends. You will feel all kinds of negative emotions if you have an abortion such as anger, depression, suicidal thoughts, fear etc.

You don't know the future so don't make assumptions about it because that can cause you to have an abortion. For the rest of your life you may end up wondering what your child would have looked like or sounded like, or felt to hold. Abortion can ruin relationships with friends and family if they knew you were going to have an abortion but didn't stop you.

A, aged 29

One woman wrote this powerful poem:

To my daughter

I would have touched your silken skin
And felt the tight grip of your fist
And seen your eyes strain to find brightness
I would have loved you.

But I gave into weakness
And rejected the gift of your little life
Not allowing myself to know its wonder and perfection.
How I long to turn back time.

To see you grow and take first steps
To smile at me and call my name

To hear your cry and meet your need
To touch you and feel your caress.

My little girl, my little love
One day we'll meet
For God forgives your mother's sin
And in his grace takes care of you.

Dear God please soothe my longing pain
Please heal me, calm me deep within.
Please let me know the future holds
Not emptiness, loss and barrenness.

I cannot, will not, replace a life
Alone that I have never known
In full fruition here and now
But I will call her by her name
She was my child; she is my love.

S, aged 23

Chapter 5

Beauty for ashes

What does it mean to work through the issue of abortion within the context of the Christian faith?

to bestow on them a crown of beauty
instead of ashes,
the oil of gladness
instead of mourning
and a garment of praise
instead of a spirit of despair (Isaiah 61:3).

In the previous chapter, I described how crushing it can be for those who make a powerful connection with a past abortion to live under the burden of feeling that they have done something unforgiveable. Sadly, in some situations this is also the message that women receive from their churches and the wider Christian community. People often arrive at our courses with their pain visibly written on their faces. Nicky-Sue often reflects that beauty is restored as the women work through the issues. The more they are able to process, the more beautiful they become. That is something I have also seen: a beauty appears and a lightness is restored. This happens as individuals approach the throne of grace and work through terrifyingly difficult issues at the foot of the cross. As the burden is lifted, life in all its fullness begins to flow again. But this process is not easy.

Our post-abortion courses are unusual in that nearly all who attend have a Christian faith. Our admissions procedure is mainly through our church in London and via the church website, where the course is advertised. As we usually have sufficient numbers to fill each course to capacity, we have never felt the need to advertise further. Not everyone attending is a member of the church; women from all over London, and even cities a commuter distance from London, have attended our courses over the years. We feel that we can offer a course for Christians, which will openly deal with faith issues, alongside other centres who offer courses with less emphasis on faith.

In this chapter I would like to reflect on some of the deeper issues surrounding abortion in relation to the Christian faith and forgiveness that may be of assistance to those in positions of pastoral leadership in churches. This information may be useful when praying through the issue with someone who wishes to receive help and counselling for a past abortion.

Why can Christians struggle to receive forgiveness?

Christians know and understand that they serve a loving God who will forgive anything taken to him in repentance. Therefore, in theory, it ought to be easy to approach God to ask for forgiveness for a past abortion. Perhaps if someone has not had any major issues to deal with in their own life, it might be hard for them to understand why the issue of forgiveness can be so complicated. Some people may think: surely all that is needed is a brief and simple prayer and then it will be possible to move on. In some cases this may be possible, but the past can be extremely complicated to untangle in practice. As I mentioned in the last chapter, I am sometimes asked: "Why is it that I don't *feel* forgiven?"

Accountability – being truthful with the past

One of the stages on the post-abortion course focuses on accountability. Those on the course are asked to identify all whom they felt were involved in their abortion experience. They then allocate proportions of responsibility to each of these people in the form of a pie chart. This is a very personal exercise. The purpose is not to blame others, but to try to draw out – from what are sometimes very complicated situations – the reality of each person's accountability towards God.

Before doing this exercise, it is not uncommon for women or men to take on all responsibility for the decision, or conversely, to put it all onto their partner or others involved – such as parents. The truth of the matter is that abortion is a common practice in our culture and is widely accepted. Each and every abortion involves many individuals, including medical professionals, abortion counsellors and the whole legal and educational structure in our society. Parents and friends can sometimes play a key part, and an individual's own attitudes and values are important too. When it comes to unravelling the issue of accountability for a past abortion, strong emotions from the past can begin to surface. These emotions can cloud the past and it may even be too painful to process honestly.

Making a list of all those who are perceived as accountable or involved in the decision can be a strangely liberating experience for someone being counselled, and can help them see their situation realistically. It helps them to sort out in their own minds what they need to take to God in repentance, and where they need to forgive others.

There are two extreme positions that those being counselled can take. The first is to accept too little responsibility, and the second is to accept too much. If they take on too little responsibility, forgiveness will only go so far. If they take on too much, then they are accepting responsibility for the behaviour of others and may not feel forgiven at the end of the process. They may therefore retain feelings of resentment towards others involved in the abortion.

Rather than definitive answers, what is needed is a willingness to engage with the issues and wrestle with them honestly. For example, in one small group we ran, none of the women felt able to give accountability to others. One did feel that the father was responsible to some extent, but she did not want to forgive him. Each felt strongly that they personally had made the decision and had chosen not to interact with others in the decision-making process. Therefore, they all felt fully responsible for the decision. Most of them still moved forward on the course, but they missed out on the freedom that can come from forgiving other people associated with the abortion.

What we are asking people to do is not simply to colour in a segment in a pie chart, rather to stand before God and be held accountable for what has taken place. This is a truly frightening step to take, especially given the associated emotion, the painful memories from the past, strong feelings of shame, an almost overpowering feeling of loss, and (as is the case in all of us) a strong natural instinct to either blame others, or at least to avoid taking responsibility oneself. In addition, for Christians there can be a fear that in facing God they may find that abortion is actually the unforgiveable sin. (This is of course completely untrue, but this is what someone's subconscious may be telling them.) The underlying fear is: what if after doing all this, God rejects me anyway?

Given the difficulties, how can we help people sort this out? When we started the course one of our helpers, Dr Mauve White, spoke on two passages from Luke's gospel: Luke 8:40–47, and Luke 7:36–50. Her insight has formed the basis of our discussions since.

Jesus heals a sick woman – Luke 8:40–47

Now when Jesus returned, a crowd welcomed him, for they were all expecting him. Then a man named Jairus, a synagogue leader, came and fell at Jesus' feet, pleading with him to come to his house because his only daughter, a girl of about twelve, was dying.

As Jesus was on his way, the crowds almost crushed him. And a woman was there who had been subject to bleeding for twelve years, but no one could heal her. She came up behind him and touched the edge of his cloak, and immediately her bleeding stopped.

"Who touched me?" Jesus asked.

When they all denied it, Peter said, "Master, the people are crowding and pressing against you."

But Jesus said, "Someone touched me; I know that power has gone out from me."

Then the woman, seeing that she could not go unnoticed, came trembling and fell at his feet. In the presence of all the people, she told why she had touched him and how she had been instantly healed. Then he said to her, "Daughter, your faith has healed you. Go in peace."

In this passage we learn that a woman had been suffering from perpetual bleeding. Under Jewish law, if a woman was bleeding this meant that she was ceremonially unclean, and therefore not allowed into the presence of others. We read that the woman had been bleeding for many years; she would probably have been made to live outside her town or village as a result. As the story unfolds we learn that Jesus was walking along in the midst of a large crowd in the middle of the town. The woman is nearby, so she must have disguised herself to mingle with the crowd (she would have been known in the local community and had she been seen she would have been driven away). Perhaps she took a cloak and wrapped it around herself. She was in a perilous position.

She had heard that Jesus brought healing and she wanted what he had. In her desperation she must have thought, "I will just step towards him. If I can touch the hem of his cloak that will make me clean. I won't ask him, I won't speak with him because I could be in serious trouble."

She managed to hide in the crowd, draw near to Jesus and touch the hem of his gown. Suddenly, she was healed. It was a miracle. Perhaps she felt something – a surge of healing power, because Jesus tells us that he felt the power going out of him. Then, disaster: Jesus stopped. He said, "Who touched me?" At that point the woman was in acute danger. Everyone was turning around looking for the person who touched Jesus, but she couldn't run away because that would draw attention to herself. If she was discovered she might be stoned. She feels alone, exposed and in danger. Eventually she decided to own up to Jesus and revealed herself to him in what must have been the most terrifying moment of her life. She knew she had been healed, but to those in the crowd she was still an object of condemnation.

This is what it can be like to stand before Jesus and repent of a past abortion. It can be terrifying. What if he rejects you? What if there is no forgiveness for abortion? What if the crowd (fellow Christians) reject you and cast you out (of the church or their friendship or their respect)?

However, what we see from the passage is that what is important is not what the crowd thinks, but Jesus' approach to the situation. Jesus knows that the woman's faith has healed her and made her clean, and he sends her on her way: restored and in peace. Jesus' response demonstrates how Christians should help those who have been through abortion or are facing an unplanned pregnancy.

Abortion is not the unforgiveable sin. Surely Christian communities should reflect the same love and acceptance that Jesus showed to those who needed healing, whether physical or spiritual? We need to ensure that church communities become reckless dispensers of his grace, not miserly doorkeepers of it, demanding repentance on their own terms. It is vital that the language used reflects the grace of God and is not judgmental or condemning. Actions must be consistent with faith. Over the years I have heard many appalling stories of people being thrown out of congregations or asked to leave a church when a pregnancy outside marriage or an abortion became known. In general, this is a wholly unacceptable action that paradoxically breeds a culture of shame and secret abortions within these churches. As a man leading this ministry, I have also noticed that if there is a fallout after an abortion, then the woman is usually blamed more than the man involved.

Christians need to be accepting and understanding of people in the difficult circumstance of an unplanned pregnancy (even if it ends with an abortion), and those who have been through abortion in the past. Remembering that we are part of a culture in which abortion is the norm, we need to be understanding and show compassion regarding the reasons why people choose abortion. Women have abortions for a wide range of reasons and do so from a point of crisis for which life has probably not prepared them. **Above all, we need to ensure that our churches do not contribute to the problem by breeding a culture of condemnation and judgment that leads to secret abortions, because people are not free to own up to mistakes or admit to past problems.**

Barriers to accepting forgiveness

There can be a paradoxical unwillingness among those we counsel to accept that God's forgiveness is free and unconditional. Like the scene from the television show *Candid Camera*, where a man stands in a crowd offering genuine £20 notes for free, but gets no takers, we suspect a trick. Perhaps there is a hidden cost; maybe the price will prove to be too high. Perhaps God will demand too much of us in return – sending us off as missionaries to somewhere unpleasant, or demand we remain single or childless or something worse. We fail to understand the sheer recklessness of God – that his grace really is free and it's ours for the taking.

There can also be a veneer of respectability. We fear facing who we really are, because that would mean admitting that we are weak or flawed. Maybe some choose not to forgive themselves so they can continue punishing themselves. Perhaps we also fear being 'damaged goods', accepted in God's kingdom only as second-class citizens, second to the wholesome Christians we see around us. Nothing could be further from the truth.

Jesus anointed by a sinful woman – Luke 7:36–50

When one of the Pharisees invited Jesus to have dinner with him, he went to the Pharisee's house and reclined at the table. A woman in that town who lived a sinful life learned that Jesus was eating at the Pharisee's house, so she came there with an alabaster jar of perfume. As she stood behind him at his feet weeping, she began to wet his feet with her tears. Then she wiped them with her hair, kissed them and poured perfume on them.

When the Pharisee who had invited him saw this, he said to himself, "If this man were a prophet, he would know who is touching him and what kind of woman she is—that she is a sinner."

Jesus answered him, "Simon, I have something to tell you."

"Tell me, teacher," he said.

"Two people owed money to a certain moneylender. One owed him five hundred denarii, and the other fifty. Neither of them had the money to pay him back, so he forgave the debts of both. Now which of them will love him more?"

Simon replied, "I suppose the one who had the bigger debt forgiven."

"You have judged correctly," Jesus said.

Then he turned toward the woman and said to Simon, "Do you see this woman? I came into your house. You did not give me any water for my feet, but she wet my feet with her tears and wiped them with her hair. You did not give me a kiss, but this woman, from the time I entered, has not stopped kissing my feet. You did not put oil on my head, but she has poured perfume on my feet. Therefore, I tell you, her many sins have been forgiven—as her great love has shown. But whoever has been forgiven little loves little."

Then Jesus said to her, "Your sins are forgiven."

The other guests began to say among themselves, "Who is this who even forgives sins?"

Jesus said to the woman, "Your faith has saved you; go in peace."

In this second passage we learn that an important and religious man invited Jesus into his house. In those days if you visited the house of a wealthy or important person, a servant would wash your feet on arrival. If you were an important guest, the host would wash your feet himself. You would be greeted, offered refreshment and oil would be rubbed into your hair; your every need would have been attended to. The host in the story obviously felt he was a bit above Jesus. He was either getting other people to practise hospitality for him, or not doing it at all. He is appalled that a 'fallen woman' sits weeping at Jesus' feet.

We learn that the fallen, weeping woman was higher in Jesus' eyes than the outwardly 'clean' religious man sitting next to him. The woman knew her need of Jesus and had a deep love for him. In an incredible act of worship and supplication she shows her love and immense gratitude for the gift of forgiveness that Jesus has given her. In return, Jesus shows he loves and understands her.

"… her many sins have been forgiven – as her great love has shown. But whoever has been forgiven little loves little" (Luke 7:47).

I once heard Jackie Pullinger (a missionary who works with drug addicts and the poor in Hong Kong) speak about her work. In her church there is an extraordinary mix of wealthy people and poor street people. Once, a wealthy businessman asked Jackie if his teenage children could work with her helpers ministering to the street people and drug addicts during the holidays. One of the team leaders took the teenagers out on to the streets.

At the end of the first day Jackie asked them how they had got on. They replied that they had been really impressed with the team leader, who had told them his story during the day. This man had been living on the streets as a drug addict and had, as a gang member, committed major crimes. He had served time in jail and along the way had become a committed Christian. They said that it was so difficult for them to understand their own personal need for Jesus: they came from good backgrounds and didn't have to deal with the harsh realities of life on the streets. But this man had gone to a depth in his faith that they could only imagine. His desperate need had opened his heart in a way that the teenagers longed for. One of them commented, "We wish we had been drug addicts. Then we would have realised our need for Jesus so much more. We are jealous of those on the streets, the criminals and the gang members whose faith is more than ours." Like the woman in the story, the gang member was able to get closer to Jesus than the respectable teachers of the law, or those who cannot see their true need of a saviour.

Finding freedom

That story of the woman weeping at the feet of Jesus in Luke Chapter 7 strikes a cord with me when I reflect on my own journey. As I sat before the cross in sorrow and repentance for my girlfriend's past abortion, I experienced something of God's heart and the depth of his forgiveness. I am now free to leave the past behind, renewed in my faith to a fullness and closeness to God that I could not have imagined when I first surrendered my heart to him.

Time after time we have seen this happen on our course. People able to resolve a past abortion can find a new and deeper faith than they imagined possible. For me, as is the case for many others, the journey took some time and was painful at times – there were a few things God wanted me to deal with on the way. But at the end there is an extraordinary peace – a new life.

In some Christian circles there is a culture that pressures people to say a quick prayer of repentance and move on. With the issue of a past abortion it can be more complicated. Moving on may well be a process that takes time and requires encouragement along the way. It is therefore imperative to allow those who have been through abortion to journey at their own pace along the path towards forgiveness, rather than expecting it to happen at once. Individuals will know when they have got there. It is more important for people to be willing to wrestle with unanswered questions, than to say a simplistic prayer of repentance and expect this to be enough.

Psalm 32:1–5 reflects much of the journey that those on our courses take:

Blessed is the one
whose transgressions are forgiven,
whose sins are covered.

Blessed is the one
whose sin the Lord does not count against them
and in whose spirit is no deceit.

When I kept silent,
my bones wasted away
through my groaning all day long.

For day and night
your hand was heavy on me;
my strength was sapped
as in the heat of summer.
Then I acknowledged my sin to you
and did not cover up my iniquity.
I said, "I will confess
my transgressions to the Lord."
And you forgave
the guilt of my sin.

Forgiving others

CS Lewis said, "Everyone says forgiveness is a lovely idea until they have something to forgive."[17] Those asking God for forgiveness for an abortion are immediately confronted with the question of forgiving the other people involved. For a woman, it might be particularly difficult to forgive the man who fathered the child. This dynamic is discussed more fully in the following chapter on men and abortion. Women might be trying to forgive the man involved at the same time as working out who was responsible for what, and experiencing powerful emotions of shame, anger and loss.

How do we ask God to come into situations where we find it hard to forgive others? How can we forgive when we do not feel that we even want to? In our heads we may be saying, "Father, forgive," but what if our hearts still feel angry or hurt?

Corrie ten Boom's book *The Hiding Place* tells the story of her life. It contains a passage I have always found helpful.[18] Corrie was in the Dutch resistance during the Second World War. She was discovered by the Gestapo and imprisoned with her sister Betsie in Ravensbruk concentration camp. Betsie was treated very badly and died in the camp, but Corrie was released in December 1944. At the end of the war she toured churches in Holland and Germany preaching forgiveness and reconciliation.

Her autobiography tells of a time not long after the end of the war when Corrie was at a church service in Germany. She had preached on forgiveness, and a queue of people formed wanting to ask her questions at the end of the service. She looked up and saw a man she recognised in the queue: he was one of the former guards from Ravensbruk This particular man had beaten her sister Betsie. She describes how in a flash she saw a heap of clothes and pile of shoes, her sister standing naked and ashamed in front of this horrific and cruel man with a whip dangling at his side.

The man spoke to Corrie without recognising her, "You mentioned Ravensbruk in your talk. I was a guard there," he said. He had become a Christian, he told her, and had received forgiveness from God, but he asked for forgiveness from her. "I know that God has forgiven me for the cruel things I did there, but I would like to hear it from your lips as well. Fräulein," the man said, stretching out his hand. "Will you forgive me?" he asked. As Corrie listened to the question all she could see was the skin pulled tight across the Betsie's ribs.

The book relates what happened next:

> "I stood there with a coldness clutching at my heart. But forgiveness is not an emotion, I knew that. Forgiveness is an act of the will and the will can function regardless of the temperature of the heart.
>
> 'Jesus help me', I prayed. 'I can lift my hand, I can do that much but you have to supply the feeling.' So I held my hand woodenly, mechanically in front of me. As I did an incredible thing took place. A current of electricity started in my shoulder, ran down my arm and sprang into the joined hands. Then this healing warmth spread throughout my body and flooded my very being. Tears sprang into my eyes.
>
> 'I forgive you brother!' I cried, 'With all of my heart!' And for a long moment we stood there with our hands clasped – a former guard and a former prisoner. I have never known God's love as intensely as I did then."

It may not seem natural to forgive those who have caused us pain, but to be able to do so can bring extraordinary rewards within the fullness of a relationship with Jesus Christ. As Corrie ten Boom says, it does not have to be an act of the emotions: above all it is an act of the will. All that is necessary is to release others to God, and leave the judging to him. God knows what happened. It may take time, but to not forgive means that ties with the past cannot be broken and may continue to have a hold on the present. As Corrie ten

Boom's story illustrates, if the words proclaiming forgiveness can be spoken, the feelings may follow later.

Forgiving others does not mean that the people involved do not need to ask for forgiveness from God themselves. What is important is for individuals to release others to God for their own sake. Neither does forgiving others mean that their actions did not matter or are something that can easily be forgotten.

Sometimes there can be a tendency for those we counsel to justify the actions of the other people involved. Someone may say, "They didn't understand," or, "They had their own issues and this is why they handled the situation badly." This too can be unhelpful. What is important is to have a realistic view, and to accept that others bear their own responsibility for their actions.

Finding fullness of faith

What, then, does it mean to explore abortion within the context of the Christian faith? I have three hopes for those working through a past abortion. First, that they will find peace and healing. Second, that they will either manage to avoid the situation of an unplanned pregnancy in future, or at least be able to make a different decision if they find themselves in the same situation again. Third, that those who are Christians will be able to reconcile this area of their life with their faith. I have noticed that abortion can be very corrosive to faith. Christians who have abortions feel that perhaps they have lost their chance of salvation, and frequently become distant from their faith and other Christians. Others feel that there is a barrier between themselves and God that prevents them from praying. It is the greatest reward for us to see people reconnect with their faith on the course, and emerge with a greater understanding of God's grace and purpose for their lives. One woman said, "Apart from becoming a Christian, this is the most significant thing I have done in my life."

The people we have met on our courses had their abortions mainly because they were unprepared for what life threw at them. They had little understanding of the risks they faced and little understanding of abortion and the potential consequences. I believe that it would be helpful if all Christians could gain an understanding of the issues and engage with the subject, at least to a level that might keep them out of an abortion clinic themselves. Most of the people on our courses were against abortion *until* they became unexpectedly pregnant. About half had their abortions when they were Christians, about half before they came to faith. None of us knows how we will react in a crisis. In an unplanned pregnancy situation it is all too easy to journey towards an abortion clinic. In Chapter 8 I will lay out what I believe are the lessons that can be learned from our course, and the issues for individuals to understand in order to avoid an abortion in their own lives.

This chapter ends with a story of God's love for one of the women on our course.

An inspiring story

Margaret O'Hara led one of our courses, as part of which there was a Saturday session. Margaret invited us to her home, and then to go with her to her local church the next day. As we drove down the hill to the church, one of the women said, "Wait, I know this place, I've been here before." She told of how many years previously, she had been in great turmoil when she discovered she was pregnant. She was a committed Christian and the daughter of a senior church leader.

At the time of her pregnancy she felt that she could not talk to her father about it in case it put him in a difficult position. As she was thinking about having an abortion, she was driving along a motorway when she saw the spire of a church. She pulled off at the next junction to find the church and pray about her situation. She entered the church building and as she started to pray she felt God tell her not to have the abortion. But she went ahead and had been carrying the guilt for many years.

The church Margaret took us to was the very same one the young woman had stopped at to pray all those years ago. She was filled with an unspeakable joy that spoke to her of absolute redemption and restoration. That God should lead her back to the same place gave her a personal reassurance that he had been with her all the time; that he had never let her go in spite of what she had done. When we met up the following week her face shone with absolute radiance. Here was a woman at peace!

This is just one story of God's grace towards a woman who had an abortion. It shows us where God is in the abortion debate: alongside those who are having abortions, calling them to choose differently beforehand, but ready to pick up the pieces afterwards. It also shows us where the church could be: standing alongside pregnant women as they wrestle with their situation and choices, and being there with arms outstretched whatever decision they may make.

Our ministry of post-abortion recovery works because at its centre is the hope and reconciliation found in Jesus Christ. He is at the heart of everything we do and only through him is full healing and restoration possible. This is why the church has such a vital role to play and why it could be so effective in offering this truth to our society, thus bringing about real change. This will not come through judging those who have been through abortion or even by campaigning for better laws, but by communicating effectively, living out true values in our own lives and by bringing God's love to those in need. This is the model that could form our response to the issue of abortion.

Chapter 6

Men and abortion

What does abortion have to do with men?

In a discussion with a Church of England curate who was planning a sermon on abortion, I mentioned the fact that up to a third of the men and women in his congregation could have experienced abortion. "*Men?*" he replied, "What has abortion got to do with men? Surely it is a women's issue?" His comment was a very telling one, and reflects the widely held view in our society that abortion is solely 'a women's issue'. The slogan 'a woman's right to choose' has no doubt underpinned this belief, but what does this 'right to choose' mean to those women who have experienced a crisis pregnancy? Conventional wisdom might suppose that when a woman discovers that she is unintentionally pregnant, she collects information on her options and then makes the decision about the pregnancy. In practice, however, from our experience of running courses for both men and women we believe that there is often another dynamic at play behind the scenes.

When it comes to making a decision, some women will have a secret abortion without consulting the man involved, and some men will coerce a woman into having an abortion against her will. Some women are determined to have an abortion regardless of what view the man holds. However, more generally the experience of the women on our courses shows that a woman will nearly always go to the man involved, tell him she is pregnant and ask him what he thinks they should do as a couple. The reply often heard is: "I will do whatever *you* want to do."

At face value this sounds supportive, but in reality it is not. The day we identified this as being an important dynamic in the decision-making process, Nicky-Sue emerged from leading the women's group looking thoughtful. She said that when one of the women had told her boyfriend that she was pregnant, he had responded by saying, "I'll do whatever you want to do". At the time the woman had thought this was very supportive, but in light of his subsequent behaviour she realised that what he was really saying was: "I'll do whatever you want to do *as long as you have the abortion*". She came to view that statement as manipulative and self-centred.

We have since discussed this in detail with the men on our course and the majority admit to understanding exactly what they were doing when they said "anything you want". They were deliberately putting the ball back in their partner's court, leaving the woman to make the decision alone, which almost certainly meant an abortion.

The following is a model answer that I have written to the question, "I am pregnant. What do you think we should do?" This answer is based on many years of talking through the issue within the women's group. Although it might be unrealistic to expect most men in this situation to actually give this answer, it is one that I believe illustrates the hidden issues behind the pregnancy, and is one that might be helpful to a woman with a crisis pregnancy. When I read this answer out on the course, it helps many to see more clearly the situation they were in, and it can come as a powerful and healing revelation to those women who felt that the responsibility for making the decision rested solely on their shoulders.

It is not just a question of providing more options or a solution; it is a question of a man offering a woman an engaged answer, something she can work with and build on as she struggles with her situation. The key issue in this illustration is not so much the commitment to the relationship; it is the commitment to the child.

She says, *"I'm pregnant, what do you think we should do?"*

He says, *"I can understand why you might decide to have an abortion, but if you wish to have the child I will stand behind you and support you in whatever way I can. If you feel you could not cope, then it might even be possible for me to take the child and raise him or her on my own if that is what you want. However, if we really feel that neither of us could cope, we could consider adoption as an option. I don't know where our relationship will go, but I am prepared to work with you and I believe that with a bit of goodwill and hard work we can get through this together."*

Even if a man did give this answer, it does not follow that the woman would necessarily choose to continue with the pregnancy, but at the very least she might feel that she had a realistic choice.

Saying "I want you to have an abortion" would be more honest, but it is not what men say. Perhaps, in their own eyes, saying "whatever you want" absolves them of responsibility. To say what they are honestly thinking might mean accepting responsibility. However, in reality, by men saying, "whatever you want", and trying to be neutral, we believe that they are strongly influencing the decision. If they really wanted to be involved with the raising of the child they could have a tremendous influence on the woman's decision. In our experience, we believe that men fully understand this at some level. They understand that saying "whatever you want" is a strong vote for abortion.

On several occasions I have had discussions with men whose partners want to have an abortion against their wishes. Legally, men are powerless to prevent an abortion and they often appear angry or distraught. Some of these men are genuinely appalled that the pregnancy will end the life of their child. With others, however, I wonder if other factors may be at work.

The power of decision-making can play into the dynamics of a relationship, with a man wishing to prove a point or assert his will over a woman. In such cases I wonder whether, if the woman decided the other way and wished to keep the child, the man would conversely demand an abortion.

I once counselled a couple where the woman felt under pressure from the man involved to have an abortion. After speaking to him, he gradually changed his mind and agreed to the continuation of the pregnancy. However, as soon as he had made this decision, the woman opted for an abortion. Perhaps she felt free to make her decision only when she knew that the man would support her either way, but in this instance other dynamics outside the pregnancy were possibly at play within the relationship.

Sometimes, in Christian circles, a man can protest loudly to make himself look better to others. His protests may only have started once the woman had safely made the abortion decision.

This is a complex area; I am not saying that all men are heartless and unfeeling. During a crisis pregnancy some men may see their role as being the one who keeps a clear head. As the battle between a woman's head and heart erupts and she swings between keeping the child or choosing abortion, the man may feel he should keep her focused on abortion as being the logical and compassionate option, one that genuinely offers a choice for the woman. Perhaps abortion plays to people's weaknesses and fears, but this does not alter the fact that men play a significant role in an abortion decision.

A difference between men and women

As we have seen, a very striking feature of the course is the anger that can surface on the first evening from women, mainly directed at the men by whom they became pregnant. As a man, it can be uncomfortable to be in the room when this anger is expressed.

To help understand the cause of this anger, it can be helpful to think of our expectations of the opposite sex: how we expect them to behave towards us. A useful question to ask in this instance is: *what is the difference between men and women?*

We have had fascinating and robust discussions around this subject on our course over the years. Interestingly there is only one statement that I have been able to produce on this subject with which nearly everyone, both men and women, would agree:

Men have a deep instinct to protect women and children. Women have a deep instinct to be protected by men.

The men and women tell us that in a crisis, a woman will look to a man for protection, and a man will instinctively want to protect her. He has an innate instinct to take responsibility for her, although a desire by men to take responsibility for a crisis pregnancy will be lacking in many relationships. (That is not to say that a woman cannot make a decision or defend herself, but at some level women generally want men to show leadership, decisiveness and courage when confronted by an external threat or a crisis.)

Perhaps men also have an instinct to protect themselves from accountability or sacrificial responsibility. So, although initially a woman can think a man's response of "whatever you want" is supportive, subsequently she may come to see this answer as a conscious withdrawing of the man's natural protection from her, and as a betrayal. She may also feel that he is not protecting the child, as she instinctively wants to, even if she eventually chooses an abortion. This sense of betrayal is the powerful source of the anger that a woman can feel after an abortion.

Women often describe being distraught after the abortion, and that the father of the child was not supportive or understanding. A woman can also be angry towards the man involved for seemingly being able to move on without showing any doubt or regret about the decision afterwards.

The effects of abortion on men

Although fewer men than women have attended our post-abortion courses, we have seen that they can be affected by abortion in exactly the same ways. Everything written about the dynamics of abortion and its effects on women in the previous chapters is equally applicable to men. They can encounter the same feelings and experience the same effects. Perhaps the point is most easily illustrated by the fact that we use *exactly* the same course for both men and women.

As with women, we believe not all men are adversely affected by an abortion in any obvious way, but many are, and the effects of abortion on men are well known and attested.[19] We have helped men overcome the same problems including, on one occasion, an eating disorder connected to a past abortion.

There may be some nuanced differences, but basically men and women go through the same healing process. With the realisation that he could have been a father of a living child, a man can come to see his behaviour as a cowardly act, abandoning his child and the woman to abortion. This can weigh heavily on him and he may come to see himself as having failed as a protector, as a provider or as a man. In turn, this may influence his self-confidence and his ability to commit to relationships.

If the abortion took place within marriage or in a committed on-going relationship it is sometimes helpful for both the woman and the man to go through a healing process separately. This is to enable them to find their own way to process their thoughts and feelings before attempting to communicate and discuss it at a meaningful level as a couple.

Who made the decision? Accountability for men

So, how do men reflect on their responsibility for a past abortion? They seem to find the idea of being held accountable for an abortion uncomfortable and will go to extraordinary lengths to avoid engaging with the subject. Just as with Adam's denial in the Garden of Eden, when he said, "The woman you put in here with me – she gave me from the tree and I ate" (Genesis 3:12), so some men seek to absolve themselves of any responsibility. They say that the pregnancy was the woman's fault; therefore the abortion decision must be hers alone. "It's her body, it was her decision," is a typical response at the beginning of a men's course. But how does this sit with women and with the innate male instinct to protect women and children?

As they look back on their decisions, most of the women on our courses believe that men were at least as accountable for the decision as they were. At some level, many women even feel that the failure of the man to protect them boxed them into a corner where they perceived they had no option, and so ultimately the man bore equal, if not more, responsibility for the decision.

Every journey begins with a first step. The journey to an abortion clinic does not just begin with the discovery of a pregnancy. It starts with a man and a woman sleeping together, and it is here that men must also accept responsibility: for their behaviour towards women, in their values, their understanding of contraception and their understanding of abortion. These are not just 'women's issues'; they are men's issues too, and whatever the story, men should be encouraged to face up to their part in an abortion decision.

A powerful illustration

I was once on holiday northwest of Vancouver Island in Canada. In a bar one night a fisherman told me a story that I believe to be true, although I have been unable to verify it. In any case, the story is a powerful illustration.

A group of friends went fishing and one of the men brought along his young son. The area where they were fishing was remote and could only be reached by trekking on foot through a forest. It was also dangerous: they were going to be fishing for salmon in a fast-flowing river where it joined the sea. If anyone fell into the river they would be swept out to sea and would either drown, or freeze in the cold water before help could reach them.

Although the father warned his son to be careful and tried to keep a watch on him, the boy hooked a large fish, became excited and slipped and fell into the freezing torrent. He screamed for help as he was carried down the rapids and into the fast-flowing current going out to sea. The father kicked off his boots, turned to his friends and said he was going after him. His friends tried to hold him back, thinking he was going to throw his life away needlessly, that rescue would not be possible. The man broke free and jumped in the water. His last words were, "I don't want him to die alone and afraid."

The father had almost certainly calculated that if he could reach his son, the boy would die of hypothermia first because he had the smaller body. It was the only gift he could give his son – not to die alone and afraid. The father swam to him and although they made it to a piece of driftwood, to which the father was able to strap them with his belt, they were swept out to sea where both died of hypothermia. Their bodies were found the following day by rescuers, the boy held tight in his father's arms with a look of peace on his face, as if he were sleeping.

The story had a powerful effect on me as it connected with what I had been thinking about the issue of abortion. In many ways, this story is the opposite of what happens in an abortion. It is a story of a father giving everything for his child, whereas the majority of abortions are the result of both men and women being unable, or unwilling, to do so.

For many men, abortion comes out of the blue. Unlike many women, most men will have never thought about abortion until a pregnancy is discovered. A crisis pregnancy is a complicated situation and there are no simple answers. Men and women communicate in very different ways and a woman will often take a man's first reaction as being the most important, whereas men generally need time to consider their position, and can change their views with time.

Abortion is not always a man's fault, and men are not generally unfeeling and cruel. However, abortion can play to self-interest and expose a lack of commitment in a relationship. We hope that men will come to understand that by remaining passive they leave women in a place where they feel they have no other choice.

My hope for any men reading this chapter is that they will be empowered to think and act differently if a partner approached them one day and said, "I am pregnant what do you think we should do?" My hope also is that both men and women will engage with and understand the causes of unintended pregnancy, and be prepared to let this knowledge influence their behaviour and choices – both within and outside marriage or a long-term relationship.

Chapter 7

Women and abortion

What is meant by 'choice'?

When we first started running our courses for women I was amazed at some of the deep and profound issues that the women themselves would raise and wish to discuss. As I have seldom heard these issues mentioned outside of our groups – not in books, the media or in conversation – I would like to reflect these issues in this chapter.

What are the perceived and actual choices?

Many of the women described to us how they felt pressured into choosing abortion. Perhaps in thinking about abortion in terms of 'choice' before a pregnancy (for example, "a woman's right to choose" or being "pro-choice"), a woman assumes that she would have a genuine choice were it needed. But when she finds herself unexpectedly pregnant, she may feel in reality that there is no other choice apart from abortion.

At first glance, the slogan "a woman's right to choose" sounds positive as it appears to offer *more* choice. However, in our culture today, the almost universal promotion of abortion as the solution for an unplanned pregnancy has effectively inhibited the development of alternative support structures that might encourage a woman to give birth. Without such support structures a woman can feel boxed into a corner and in no position to continue with the pregnancy. In our culture today what is meant by "choice" for the majority is effectively the sole choice of an abortion. But what about women who would rather be pregnant and continue with the pregnancy? Where is their choice? Where is the unconditional support of a partner and of society?

Some women on the course tell us that their perceived lack of choice contributed to the pressure they felt when they found themselves with an unintended pregnancy. As the pregnancy progresses, the head-heart dilemma described in Chapter 2 may cause a woman's view of abortion to begin to change, even if she had always assumed she would take the abortion route. As feelings of motherhood emerge the awareness of the baby growing inside may make her yearn to continue with the pregnancy. However, the lack of a viable support structure may lead her to despair of giving birth: it seems too difficult to do on her own. She wants the support of a partner – the father of her child.

It is this perceived lack of choice that drives the strong feelings of coercion that are often described after an abortion, and this explains why so many women on our course came to feel that something cruel and nasty was done *to* them, even though, in reality, they were the ones making the abortion decision.

Nancyjo Mann (founder of the organisation Women Exploited by Abortion) says:

> "For many women, abortion is experienced not as an act of 'choice', but as an act of despair; their only choice when faced with an unplanned pregnancy.
>
> Women are being abandoned by a society which has no patience for a problem unique to women – an unplanned pregnancy. Rather than receiving the love and support needed to cope with this challenge, women are offered the easy way out, the 'quick-fix,' the cover-up: abortion.
>
> Abortion is the 'cheap love' which society offers as a substitute for costly care and honest commitment. Though offered superficial support in making their abortion decisions, women must always face the consequences alone. Abortion, unlike childbirth, is always a lonely process."[20]

Unwanted by whom?

One of the differences between men and women that we have observed on our courses is their view of what it means to be in a committed relationship. Many women on the course were surprised and angered by the lack of commitment that their pregnancy and subsequent abortion revealed in their relationships. Some were also surprised by how this undermined their ability to choose something other than abortion.

It has long been an article of faith among some feminists that abortion empowers women by giving them control over their fertility, with the mantra "every child should be a wanted child" urging that unwanted children should not be brought into the world.

But as Professor Kristin Luker puts it:

> "Unwanted by whom? Women who were having abortions in the 1970s were women who did not want to be pregnant. If you talked to people in those days, they said it was a relief. They said that it gave them something they would not otherwise have had.
>
> Today, by contrast, we are increasingly seeing a population of women who would rather be pregnant but cannot continue the pregnancies for reasons not having to do with their own volition."[21]

The feminist writer Germaine Greer said, "The goal was 'every child a wanted child'; it should also have been 'every abortion a wanted abortion.' "[22]

Without a partner's wholehearted and engaged support, many women will not feel that they are in a position to continue with a pregnancy. Many men do not offer this level of support, as their expectation is that women will choose abortion. Therefore, through their willingness to undergo abortion, women have effectively empowered men by giving them a veto over the continuation of a pregnancy. Although some women do continue with their pregnancies alone and without support, it could be argued that men now have the decision-making power over a woman's fertility, or as Nancyjo Mann says:

> "The abortion 'choice' is just one more arena in which men condition their love and respect on the basis of women's obedience to their desires."[23]

I would suggest that it would be helpful for all those in a relationship to explore what they would do as a couple should the woman become pregnant, looking at all the options available. If the man says, "whatever you want" I would encourage his partner to probe further – what exactly does he mean by that? If the woman wanted to keep the child, would the man really stand by her? Would he be prepared to be seriously involved in bringing up the child, or even take the child and raise it on his own if that was what the woman wanted? What *would* he be willing to give up?

At the beginning of a relationship we have noticed that couples may discuss contraceptive options, but never discuss abortion and what they would do in the case of an unplanned pregnancy. Both women and men need to realise that there is a very real risk of experiencing this dilemma, and it is helpful for everyone to know where they stand before a crisis presents itself.

Fertility and abortion

In contrast with previous generations, many women today delay having children, allowing other career, economic or social prospects to take priority. The average age of marriage in the UK is now 31 for women (up from 25 in 1991 and 23 in 1981).[24] The average childbearing age is now 29.5 (up from 23 in 1968).[25]

Many women will have an abortion when they are at the height of their fertility in their 20s (74% of abortions are undertaken by women aged 29 or under [26]). A woman's fertility begins to decline after the age of 30, and reduces dramatically after the age of 35.[27] In contrast, though the quality of their sperm can decline, men still retain a much higher level of fertility into their 40s, 50s, and even 60s.

On the post-abortion course we observed that women are surprisingly ill informed about their fertility prospects after the age of 30. The fact that they will be dramatically less fertile after their mid-thirties often comes as a complete surprise. Many either do not appear to understand the fragility of fertility, or choose to ignore its implications. Perhaps there is an assumption that IVF or other fertility treatment will provide options later in life but, for the majority of women with low fertility who wish to become pregnant after the age of 35, these treatments will not be successful.[28] Media stories about older mothers can also give a false impression, as these situations are not the norm.

The sad reality is that some women will abort the only child they will carry in their lifetime. For many, by the time they realise this, it is too late to do anything about it. The same is less likely for men of the same age who retain their fertility for longer and have the option of being a parent with a younger partner.

On our course, some of the women who had an abortion in their 20s were concerned about their fertility in their 30s. It seemed to us that abortion can sometimes shift the long-term balance of power in a relationship towards men, who effectively retain a veto on all reproductive decisions, and thus dictate the pace of the couple's relationship and lifestyle.

For some women, far from giving them control over their lives, it seems that abortion can leave many exposed to childlessness in the long term. It can be heart-breaking for women who had an abortion in their 20s to be unable to conceive later in life.

The hidden cost of abortion – understanding the loss

People may think of abortion in terms of gain: gaining control of their fertility, gaining control of their lives, gaining an advantage in how they live their lives. However, many women who have had abortions look back on their experience in terms of loss – a loss so great it invalidates their original decision. At the heart of this loss lies a feeling that something was unexpectedly taken away from them.

As I mentioned earlier, the most common comment we hear on the women's course is, "a part of me died that day". What is it that causes women to say this? What has been lost? In the introduction I told the story of the woman who arrived on our course dressed in black, and left embracing colour and joy.

On her last day of the course she wrote: "You have restored what was taken by the abortion; you have given me back my motherhood. I feel [like] a whole woman again." This is what abortion can take away from so many women. It can rob them of their sense of motherhood, their natural optimism and the desire to have children in the future.

Most women on our courses discover that they have been living with the sub-conscious thought *I participated in ending the life of my child* buried deep in their hearts. This has been the hardest thing to write in this book and it has taken us many years to speak these words out in public and put them in writing.

For 20 years Nicky-Sue and I avoided saying this, and on the course itself we found it extremely difficult to deal with the issues raised by this terrible truth. Try as we might to avoid any direct mention of it, the women themselves nearly always made this connection. For them, resolving this issue was the key to release and healing.

People commonly think that abortion is easier than either placing a child for adoption or bringing up a child in less than ideal circumstances. However, many of the women on our courses look back on their experience with longing – a desire to have given birth to their child and a longing to have done things differently.

It is true that, for some, hindsight comes only with the benefit of maturity and experience, and that due to circumstances some might well make the same decision even if they could wind back the clock. However, most told us that with the benefit of hindsight, and appreciating now the connection that they had made with their child prior to the abortion, they would have chosen differently. In other words, if they could go back, most would keep their child. For many, abortion was clearly seen to be the wrong choice.

In her book, *How to Be a Woman,* Caitlin Moran again writes of her personal experience of abortion. She views it in positive terms as giving her control of her life:

> "All I could see – and all I see now years later – is history made of millions of women trying to undo the mistake that could then undo them, and then just carrying on, quiet, thankful, and silent about the whole thing. What I see, is that it can be an action with only good consequences."[29]

This widely held and uncritical view of abortion that sees "only good consequences" can be dismissive of the evidence that many women experience negative consequences. Such a view is either based on ignorance, a belittling of the significance of their experience (by implying that some women have pre-existing or latent emotional or mental problems), or a paternalistic view that women who cannot cope with an abortion would certainly not be able to cope with bringing an 'unplanned' child into the world.

I see the situation differently. When I think of abortion, I think of millions of women and men condemned to live in the shadows, haunted by feelings of guilt and remorse, deeply affected and scarred by their experience of abortion. I see that for some women, abortion can be an action with only negative consequences.

I appreciate that to those brought up in a culture that overwhelming accepts abortion as a woman's right, the ability to see it in a different light can be hard.

It can be difficult to see the issues clearly. For example, surveys undertaken at abortion clinics can sometimes show high levels of satisfaction immediately after an abortion, and some women publically declare that their abortion saved their lives, that it was the best thing that happened to them. But as stated in previous chapters, a more complex picture can emerge with time for a great many women.

From our experience on the course, and in discussing the issues raised with other counsellors around the country who report similar findings, we believe that negative experiences of abortion are widespread. So why are these factors not more widely known and discussed? A solid wall of silence has grown up around the subject of abortion in our culture; there is a reluctance to discuss it in public. As well as the barriers of shame and secrecy, it can seem almost heretical to question the modern orthodoxy that abortion is best outcome for an unintended pregnancy – an affront perhaps to the rights of women.

The culture of abortion is so deeply ingrained in our society that even revealing the pain and suffering that it causes can seem, to some, a betrayal of women's rights. But given the reality of what is taking place, it does not make sense to discourage a wider discussion on the validity of abortion – a discussion that goes beyond the separate issue of whether abortion should be legal or not.

Challenging the automatic acceptance of abortion by our society does not mean denying the legal rights of those women who do want to have abortions, or suggest that access to abortion should be completely denied. Abortion is legal in the UK, and I am not advocating that it should be made illegal (which would merely result in widespread backstreet abortion). But my hope is that every woman choosing an abortion will be aware of both sides of the story, and of the potentially life-changing consequences of her choice.

Chapter 8

Shaping an effective personal view

How should Christians respond?

In this chapter I would like to suggest how individual Christians might shape an effective personal view, one to help them engage with abortion at a meaningful level, helping them avoid it in their own lives and to know what to say to friends or family about it. In the following chapter I suggest ways in which the church might respond as a community to the issue.

Where to start?

Given the widespread acceptance of abortion in our society it can seem highly counter-cultural to hold a different view, but the truth is that abortion (with the sole exception of saving a mother's life) remains incompatible with the Christian faith. To say this is not to be bigoted or judgmental, it is to hold a view that is consistent with the Bible and the overwhelming witness of Christian history and contemporary Christian belief. This view is based on an acute understanding of the issue and the consequences of abortion.

For a contemporary Christian audience engaging with the issue for the first time, perhaps the biggest stumbling block to forming a clear view is the fear that to question abortion is to be in some way *anti*-women. At a recent conference a Christian student asked me, "Can I be anti-abortion and pro-choice?" This question summed up this widespread reluctance, especially amongst young Christians, to voice doubts about abortion. The fear is that questioning abortion is tantamount to coercively imposing Christian values on others, and will result in a demand to make abortion illegal or lead to the further curtailing of women's rights.

In his book *Making Abortion Rare*, David Reardon suggests that instead of trying to make abortion illegal, Christians should focus on making it, "Unthinkable for pregnant women. Unthinkable for loved ones to whom they will turn when faced with a crisis pregnancy."[30]

Over the years, it has been seen that seeking to impose a minority view on the majority through the legal or legislative process has not brought about change. Instead, in order to transform our society's thinking on abortion I would suggest that thinking needs to be changed from the bottom up, rather than running a campaign. Everyone, including abortion providers, would agree that reducing unintended pregnancy rates is desirable, and that in an ideal world there would be no need for abortion.[31] Making abortion unthinkable is a much more practical aim, requiring a broader approach: the transformation of our culture by influencing values, thus removing the demand for abortion. This is also more achievable, because it is possible to start on a small scale by working with individuals, small groups and local church communities.

Making abortion illegal could simply create a vast market in backstreet abortion and abortion tourism, where people travel to countries where it is legal. In any event, with the advent of RU 486 (the abortion pill), it is now possible to supply a medical abortion anywhere in the world by post, thus fairly easily making illegal abortion widely available. So in many ways the legal status of abortion not relevant to the issue and I am not suggesting that abortion should be made illegal. The Christian view, however, is that abortion should be unthinkable with the sole exception of saving a mother's life.

Another stumbling point for Christians when engaging with the issue is the implication is that by questioning the "right to choose" it is the fundamental right for women to make a choice that is being questioned rather than the issue of abortion itself. To resolve this confusion it is helpful to move the issue from the abstract to the personal. The real question is not, "Should a woman have the right to choose an abortion?" But, "Would I *personally* have an abortion?" Thinking about it in this way is more balanced and brings the real issues more sharply into focus. As will be discussed later in this chapter, it is also helpful to move our thinking from the extreme to the ordinary. In reality, the most likely circumstance that an individual might face in their own life is an unintended pregnancy due to contraceptive failure or misuse. Therefore, it is most useful to think through this possibility and base a wider view of abortion on the outcome of this thinking. That is not to dismiss other, more extreme circumstances as being irrelevant to those who experience them, but in truth it is not helpful to base a belief about abortion on theoretical or abstract circumstances such as rape, which for the overwhelming majority are highly unlikely (see Appendix I for a further discussion on the issue of rape and abortion).

Shaping an effective personal view

As has been said already, it can be very tempting to see abortion as the most obvious solution to a crisis pregnancy. My heart has gone out to every individual I have met in this situation. It can be so easy to see people as an exception and to believe that, just in this case, an abortion would be the right decision. At times it can be a struggle to see the issue clearly.

John Wimber, the American founder of Vineyard Ministries, once said, "I am just a fat man trying to get to heaven". By this I think he meant that we are all sinners living in a fallen world, trying to do the right thing and attempting to make sense of the world through our faith as best we can. When it comes to abortion, allowing our faith to transform us through the renewing of our minds does not mean becoming judgmental or narrow-minded, but rather allowing our Christian faith to shape our response to a crisis and to take actions consistent with our faith. Ultimately, we may need to set aside what appears to be a 'convenient solution' and be prepared to wrestle with the complexity of the situation. If we get it wrong we know that we can always trust in the grace, mercy and love of Jesus Christ.

In my experience, some Christians think they have a clear-cut view of the subject, and that they themselves would never have an abortion. But life can turn out to be more complicated than we expect. I think of a woman who once joined our course. She had had an abortion a few years previously and wanted to explore some of the issues this had brought up for her. She was bright and intelligent and had a successful career. She had been raised in a Christian family and would have described herself as having a strong Christian faith all her life.

This young woman had one fervent passion stemming from her early teenage years: campaigning against abortion. She was horrified by abortion. She knew a lot about it and campaigned against it vigorously. She had even picketed abortion clinics, handing out leaflets to women going in for abortions. Yet, when she found herself unexpectedly pregnant, *she had an abortion.*

In 2000, a paper entitled *The Only Moral Abortion is My Abortion* was published online.[32] This international study was undertaken by an abortion clinic employee who noticed that someone who had previously been protesting outside her clinic came in to have an abortion. She mentioned this to some of her colleagues who told her similar stories from their own experience. She then corresponded with other abortion clinics around the world and collated some of the many incidents of this phenomenon.

The case studies make fascinating reading. One example tells of a mother and daughter who were both protesting outside an abortion clinic one day. The following day, the mother brought her daughter in for an abortion, and both were back on the protest line the very next day! Another woman justified her action by saying: "The only moral abortion is my abortion", prompting the title of the paper. I don't know the author personally, and it is not possible to check her sources, but from our experience, the paper's findings rings true. The complex nature of life means that people can swing from protesting outside a clinic to becoming a client all too easily.

So, there clearly seems to be a gap between the way people think about abortion and what action they actually take when crunch time comes. Having read the stories above, we may still think that this would never happen to us, but the story serves as a warning that even those who thought they had a clear-cut view may end up having an abortion.

What, then, should be the correct Christian response to this issue? I would suggest that it is this: ***that Christians should resolve not to have an abortion and to live this out as an intentional value in their own lives.***

However, given the prevalence of abortion in the culture around us, I believe that avoiding abortion requires a high degree of intentionality. It requires attaining an awareness of the risks, and taking action to avoid them. Taking the following deliberate steps would help achieve this aim.

1. Understanding that abortion is a personal issue, and that as individuals we are at risk

We may all have a stereotype in our minds of the sort of person we imagine might have an abortion. It might be a teenager or someone pregnant from a one-night stand, or perhaps someone who has had the terrible misfortune of being raped. Whatever our thoughts are about the sort of person who might have an abortion, the one person we might think it will not be is someone like *me*. We assume abortion doesn't happen to people like us, but statistically, it affects people across all sectors of society. Statistically, those who have abortions are just like you and me.

Therefore, we each need to think the issue through for ourselves, and decide beforehand what our response to a crisis pregnancy would be, either in our own lives or those of our friends or family. No one deliberately sets out to have an abortion, but the first step on the road to an abortion clinic is not having thought the issue through before a crisis. Unless we as individuals have a consistent view that shapes our behaviour and actions, we may be tempted by the wrong set of circumstances and be influenced by the decisions that many around us are making. We also need to understand the highly institutionalised nature of abortion in our society, and that most medical professionals will assume that an abortion will be desired in the case of an unintended or unwanted pregnancy.

The view that we form regarding abortion should always be expressed in a compassionate and sensitive way, with an awareness that, due to the fact that one third of women and men will have experienced abortion in our culture, in any setting there could be men and women for whom abortion is a difficult personal issue. We need to let God's grace abound in everything we say and do, and ensure that love and compassion forms the basis of our response. We must ensure that what we say does not become a stumbling block for the work of the gospel. This does not mean staying silent, but it does mean avoiding insensitive language and being prepared to think and act compassionately and with love when faced with a crisis pregnancy.

2. Understanding that the ability to control fertility is limited, even with contraception

Every year in Britain, around 750,000 live births take place, and around 200,000 conceptions are terminated by an abortion.[33]

The truly astonishing fact about these conceptions is not just the abortion rate. Rather, even though at any one time 75% of the population aged 18–44 uses contraception,[34] around 50% of all live births are unintended pregnancies.

Half of ALL live births in the United Kingdom are unintended.[35]

This situation in not only found in the United Kingdom, but also across the developed world. Professor James Trussell, director of population research at Princeton University and expert in population trends and contraception, comments on the situation in the USA:

> "What is, to me, the most mind-boggling statistic is that half (48%) of women aged 15–44 in the US have had an unintended pregnancy. So when you walk down a street in New York, half of the women will have had an unintended pregnancy."[3]

Therefore, we need to let our personal expectation of our ability to control our fertility (even if contraception is used) be shaped by the facts. In practice, we cannot always prevent conception. This fact needs to influence our decisions about our sexual relationships, both before and within marriage. Christian men, in particular, should be challenged by this fact to take responsibility for their actions. (To re-iterate the point made in Chapter 2: contraception can be highly effective if used correctly, but in practice this is not always the case, leading to the high rate of unintended pregnancy.)

When making their choices, some Christians may also not be aware that some forms of contraception may act as a form of early abortion.

3. Having open discussions with our partners

None of us know what pressures we will face in life. Christians who choose abortion may do so because they are unprepared for what life suddenly throws at them. At the beginning of a relationship, people often discuss contraception, but they rarely discuss abortion and what they would do if an unintended pregnancy were experienced. I would suggest that couples should spend time exploring their values and what they might do if faced with an unplanned pregnancy or the offer of a test for foetal abnormality, *before* they are in a potentially difficult situation. This may prevent much heartache in future.

4. Being informed about adoption

Our culture has an overwhelmingly negative view of adoption. However, from a Christian perspective adoption is a valid and compassionate resolution to an unintended pregnancy where a mother or family may not be able to cope with the arrival of a new child. Therefore, it helps to allow a positive view of adoption as an empowering alternative to abortion inform our minds, especially as adoption procedures have changed considerably over the years. To counter negative stereotypes of adoption, it might help to understand how the adoption process works today.

Adoption procedures are now very different from what they used to be. The choice of adoption can be considered by the mother at any time during pregnancy and after the child is born. It is fully accepted by adoption agencies that following the birth the mother needs time to recover and for her hormones to settle down. Any decisions made within the first six weeks of birth will not be binding. Every opportunity is given to the mother to reflect and review her decision and to be sure of her thoughts, her wishes and her feelings. Support and counselling are offered throughout to assist with this journey. In the early stages a mother may change her mind at any time, but as the adoption process develops and evolves it may take longer to be able to withdraw, especially once the child has been placed and begun the essential bonding process with a new family.

A mother's wishes and preferences concerning how they want their child adopted will be actively considered, along with what is in the best interests for the child. If a woman decides on adoption she is able to provide information about herself, the child's birth, early life and why the child was placed for adoption, if she would like to. This information is incorporated into a Life Story Book and can be given to the child in an age appropriate format by the adoption agency when the time is right. It can also be requested when a young adopted person reaches adulthood.

The Adoption and Children Act of 2002 now places a responsibility on the adoption agency to actively explore the views of the wider birth family, including the birth father and his family (if that is desired) about the new baby and whether they wish to consider adopting the child. These views are sought alongside considering an adoptive family. However, it is important to note that the birth mother is not legally obliged to name the child's father on the birth certificate.

Adoption can be a very positive option for those who truly cannot care for a child. Although relinquishing the baby can be painful, and it may be difficult at this stage to see the positives, there can be good outcomes for everyone involved.

5. Extreme circumstances

When thinking about the issue of abortion, it may be helpful not to let extreme circumstances dominate our thinking. Many feel that in some exceptional situations, such as pregnancy following rape, or an under 18 who is pregnant, abortion is an understandable and justifiable action.

However, if people accept that abortion is permissible in extreme circumstances and then find themselves in a crisis pregnancy, this may well constitute 'extreme circumstances' to them (even though it is not one of the extremes in which they thought abortion was permissible). This is the mechanism by which those who are against abortion can end up choosing it, effectively saying, "The only moral abortion is my abortion". It is the tear in the fabric of their beliefs through which they can all too easily fall.

6. Resolving a past abortion

Our experience has shown that it is also helpful for Christians to reconcile their experience within the context of their faith. For those who have been through an abortion, it can be difficult to see the issue clearly if the personal reasons why the abortion happened remain unresolved. One third of all abortions are repeat procedures; it seems to leave people vulnerable to further abortions in future. Therefore, it is helpful to think through the past in order to understand the different factors that resulted in an abortion, and to raise personal awareness in an endeavour to avoid repeating past behaviours.

While some people may be able to resolve the matter simply between themselves and God, if others wish to take it further or deeper, then post-abortion support is available in many parts of the country. Abortion can be corrosive to faith, and our experience is that Christians who go through a structured healing process can find a new faith and walk with God. This is not about public confession or testimony; it is about finding peace in our own hearts and overcoming the unhelpful sensitivities that leave individuals at risk. Diffusing personal tension regarding a past abortion can also encourage others to engage with the issue and promote a healthy and open public discussion.

Conclusion – reducing the risk of abortion in our own lives

In his book *Human Error,* Professor James Reason provides the following definition of 'error':

> "Error will be taken as a generic term to encompass all those occasions in which a planned sequence of mental or physical activities fails to achieve its intended outcome, and where these failures cannot be attributed to the intervention of some chance agency."[37]

The book draws a distinction between a slip (an unintended action), a lapse (unintended failure to act) and a mistake (intended action but unintended outcome).

Professor Reason's work has been used in the aviation world to develop the concept of "defence in depth" to minimise the risk of human error (sometimes known as the "Swiss Cheese Model"). This concept intentionally uses a mixture of skill-based, rule-based and knowledge-based behaviour (as opposed to just rule-based behaviour) to build a multi-layered defence to protect against risk.

Christians today may have very little knowledge about abortion, little skill in thinking it through themselves or discussing it with others, and only a vague understanding of Christian tradition (what Christian theologians and historians have to say on the subject). I believe that building knowledge about abortion and the creation of a safe environment where people are free to talk the issue through could add the missing dimension to Christian thinking and practice, thus preventing the behaviour that could result in an unintended pregnancy (a 'slip' or 'lapse') from turning into the regret ('mistake') of an abortion.

I would like to challenge church leaders to consider the need to impart knowledge about the Christian perspective on abortion to their congregations, and to take the lead in changing the way it is thought about and discussed. I also challenge individual Christians to engage with this subject as a matter of urgency and to take the necessary steps to avoid abortion in their own lives.

Chapter 9

Breaking the silence around abortion

Helping the world to discover the truth – how the Christian community could be key in transforming society

Due to the powerful silence that has grown up around the topic of abortion, it has become a contentious and difficult subject to talk about in public – both inside and outside the church. I believe this silence is destructive because it hides the reality of abortion in our society today. The silence prevents discussion of a number of key issues that, if they were more widely known about and understood, could be the basis for transforming our society's uncritical acceptance of abortion. These issues include:

- An understanding of how widespread it is
- The reasons for unintended pregnancy
- The effects that abortion can have on some women
- The effects that abortion can have on some men

- The role of men in the decision making process, and how women can be placed at a disadvantage in a relationship.

This silence first became apparent to me when I began speaking about abortion in small church groups. Initially I assumed that it was simply an absence of knowledge or interest that made raising the subject difficult. But I soon came to realise that the silence is deep-rooted and masks some complex issues.

What causes the silence?

Silence can be caused, either by an absence of something (for instance an absence of knowledge or sound or conversation), or by a presence of something else (such as fear, shame or dissention). I would argue that all of these elements are present in the silence surrounding abortion. What lies at its heart is a widespread desire not to be judgmental of those who choose abortion or who have experienced it in the past.

Abortion is a controversial issue. Nevertheless it is widely supported by our society. Within the church many Christians now occupy a middle ground – neither seeing it as a personal option, nor condemning others. Attempting to reconcile the position that abortion is neither right nor wrong results in a desire to avoid the subject altogether. Any mention of abortion involves making a value judgment, which may involve judging others. As the desire to avoid being judgmental is paramount, abortion is either too sensitive to talk about, or it is even as an issue that should not be spoken about in public. It can seem as if discussion of abortion has been removed from the public sphere and relegated to a matter of individual preference or 'choice'. This barrier of 'non-judgmentalism' is perhaps the largest barrier to open discussion.

Another barrier is the fact that abortion is so widespread. A high proportion of people have experienced it. Many others know family or friends who have had abortions, and quite rightly do not wish to cause offence. Some are aware of the pain that it has caused to those around them and therefore wish to maintain a protective silence. Those who have been there themselves rarely want to talk about it.

As has been stated earlier, there can be a feeling that to question abortion is to deny women a 'right', and to be in some way anti-women. As a man speaking about abortion in public I run the risk of appearing misogynistic. In the church there can also be a wariness of being associated with extreme Christian campaigning groups who conduct high-profile protests outside abortion clinics. No wonder it is such a difficult subject to discuss.

Many believe that silence and a refusal to engage with the subject is compassionate, but in reality the silence simply covers up the problem, making it difficult to make sense of what is happening around us. The silence prevents people seeking help for a past abortion and leaves everyone vulnerable to it. It also means that extreme groups remain unchallenged and this can result in unhelpful, confrontational debate if it is raised in public.

What about the church?

Within the church there is an added layer of complexity when trying to raise the subject of abortion. An absence of an engaged, compassionate theology can leave people unsure of what to say or how to react. There can also be a perceived conflict between the church's role in defending marriage and family values and being accepting of those in situations that fall outside of these desired values.

Although throughout history the church has maintained that abortion is only acceptable in order to save a mother's life, and theoretically, there is a remarkable degree of unanimity between different traditions on this point, the truth is that there is widespread sympathy and support for abortion among Christians of all denominations.

Personally, I have encountered widespread support for abortion when speaking to Christian audiences from a wide range of backgrounds and traditions. And as we have seen on our courses, many Christians from different denominations end up as clients of abortion clinics. We believe there to be a widespread culture of secret abortion among Christians today. So, what has gone wrong?

To a generation brought up to perceive abortion as a compassionate response to a crisis pregnancy, the church's concerns about when a life begins can seem theoretical, academic and remote to a woman facing the life-changing situation of an unwanted pregnancy (especially as abortion is viewed as an action without negative consequences). Overall, the traditional approach is perceived as lacking in compassion and understanding. In addition, traditional teaching can be viewed as judgmental and condemnatory when considering the position of those who have been personally involved (the use of insensitive vocabulary can make this issue particularly charged).

It is easy to understand how abortion has become a contentious subject in the church over the years, and why there is widespread dissention from traditional doctrine. As abortion is now rarely spoken about in the church, the overwhelming majority of Christians have little understanding of the subject and how to apply their faith to it. What could be done to change this?

A willingness to engage with the complexity of abortion is vital in developing the church's response to the issue. It is important for the subject to be discussed openly and honestly among church communities, outside of merely reacting to an unintended pregnancy or abortion crisis. The aim is not so much to reinforce traditional church doctrine (although this is helpful if undertaken sensitively), but for leaders to decide what type of culture they wish to nurture and promote within their churches. Ideally, it will be a culture of openness, honesty and unconditional support for those in a crisis, or who have an abortion in the past. This may include deciding how to support and encourage a woman in a crisis to continue with a pregnancy, but also being prepared to nurture and preserve the relationship even if there is a subsequent abortion.

On one of our post-abortion healing courses recently there were three women who had been expelled from their churches. Two were asked to leave when a past abortion came to light, the other when the pregnancy was discovered. I appreciate that individual circumstances can be difficult (I have heard many extreme situations over the years), but in general expelling people is an action that is unhelpful and heart-breaking for the individual, and it reinforces a culture of secrecy and silence.

In my book *Abortion – Breaking the Silence in the Church,* I outline a few simple steps that could be taken to promote an open and honest discussion within the church. In this book there is specific teaching on theology written by Dr Sean Doherty, ethics tutor at St Mellitus Theological College in London, and a suggested new model of theology based on an engaged and compassionate understanding of the issues. I am mindful that church leaders are busy people. As a result the steps suggested in the book are easy to achieve. It is not about campaigning or being anti-abortion, but rather providing care, unconditional love and acceptance and ending the silence that hides the truth.

How can the church help women (and men) who have been through an abortion?

When I speak in a church gathering women sometimes come up to me afterwards and say things like:

"It was 30 years ago, but there hasn't been a day I haven't thought about it."

"It happened 20 years ago. I still cry."

"I don't know what to do, I can't go on."

"I have never told anyone, I thought I was the only person who felt like this."

"I think I am going mad, I can't stop thinking about the abortion."

People in our churches are suffering in silence, feeling they will be condemned if they admit to a past abortion or express what they are feeling. It is essential to begin speaking in a way that will be of help to them.

The church is the one place where complete healing and restoration after an abortion is possible. While it is helpful for individuals to work through the issues, for example on a post-abortion healing course, ultimately it is reconciling the matter with God that brings peace in all its fullness. Therefore, by breaking the silence around the issue of abortion with compassion, humility and understanding, the church can become an avenue for God's grace and healing. By openly and compassionately engaging with the subject and publicly acknowledging what happens to some women (and men) after an abortion, we can help validate the suppressed feelings experienced by many, thus helping them identify these feelings and resolve the connected issues.

Another way to be of service to those who have been through an abortion is to ensure that if abortion is ever talked about in public, it is spoken about with care and sensitivity. In the past there has been a tendency among those addressing the subject of abortion in church to use unhelpful language and symbols. This is a sensitive subject, and it is important to bear in mind that there will be people in every audience who will have been directly affected by abortion.

It is important to reassure people that abortion is not the unforgivable sin (this is what many who have been through abortion believe). Some Christians who choose to have an abortion do so in the belief that they are knowingly disobeying God and this is not his best plan for them. After the abortion, the feelings of guilt that many begin to feel at the act of termination can be compounded by this awareness of disobedience, and many begin to believe they have lost their salvation. Some drift away from church and avoid their Christian friends. Some have expressed how God's calling on their life seemed to leave them after the abortion. Paradoxically, some choose to remain on the edge of their faith as a way of avoiding their true feeling about the abortion. Therefore, when it comes to forgiveness, we must become the reckless dispensers of God's grace, not his miserly doorkeepers offering forgiveness on our own terms.

As previously mentioned in the Chapter on 'men and abortion', it is important to hold men accountable as well as women. Speaking this truth out in public can come as a healing revelation to women who have been through abortion and are struggling under the illusion that they bear all the responsibility.

Sometimes I am asked, "How can I be of help to a friend who has just had an abortion?" My advice is to come alongside and be a support, but be prepared not talk about it too much. A friend may even not want to talk about it at all, in which case the best thing is to re-affirm your friendship, acceptance and support. If they are a Christian, they may be watching for rejection, so it might be helpful to state that this is not the case. If they are not a Christian they may assume you have extreme anti-abortion views, so again it might be helpful to verbalise your love and acceptance of them. Thank them for telling you. Tell them that it does not change your love for them, or your friendship.

Our experience on the post-abortion course is that the 'tunnel vision' described in Chapter 2 can last for a long time, and a person's true feelings may only start to emerge gradually. We generally recommend that people wait at least one year after an abortion before attending our course, but it might be helpful to have a one-on-one session with a counsellor if there are pressing issues that cannot wait. Do not underestimate the power of prayerful support.

How the Christian community could be key in transforming society

Martin Luther King said:

> "There was a time when the Church was very powerful. It was during that period when the early Christians rejoiced when they were deemed worthy to suffer for what they believed. In those days the Church was not merely a thermometer that recorded the ideas and principals of popular opinion; it was a thermostat that transformed the mores of society."[38]

Perhaps the greatest opportunity for Christians lies in the area of post-abortion counselling and healing, where there is a great need to bring compassion, healing and restoration to those hurting from a past abortion. This is just the area that plays to the traditional Christian strengths of love, compassion and pastoral care, and where Christians could be most effective.

When I first asked if I could start a post-abortion course at a church in London, the leaders were puzzled by my request. They thought that it might be better to start a crisis pregnancy counselling service, to help women considering abortion to review their options in a neutral environment, or help those wishing to keep their children. My view is that crisis pregnancy counselling is one side of the coin and post-abortion counselling the other, and Christian love and compassion are vital in both ministries. Many women on our courses have stated that they wished they had had access to helpful counselling before their decision, and had they done so might have chosen differently, so I can see the benefits of effective crisis pregnancy counselling. I appreciate that a post-abortion course might have thus seemed counter-intuitive and not the most obvious course of action, but when I stuck to my request they graciously assented and we have been running the courses ever since.

By listening to those who have experienced abortion, I have seen that abortion is a reflection of deeply-held values and the complex behaviour of those within our culture. Challenging the idea that abortion is the most helpful outcome for a woman with an unplanned pregnancy therefore requires an understanding of this behaviour and what happens after an abortion. I believe that understanding the connections that women and men make with their children lost through an abortion adds a dimension to our thinking: it shows us the hidden complexities and can challenge the casual acceptance of abortion by our society. This is an area where the church can play to its strengths, and perhaps one day become the thermostat that reduces the number of abortions.

Throughout this book I have explained that some women and men maintain a powerful connection with a past abortion due to strong feelings of loss and grief experienced through the loss of their child. The reason I have explained this is not an attempt to put women off abortion by implying that there is a psychological risk, but rather because I believe that understanding why women and men make this connection shows us that a human life is lost through an abortion in a way that thinking about whether a life has begun does not. If those with experience of abortion are helped by Christians and churches, I believe that this view will become widely known in church circles and will begin to influence the world around us. If we can free ourselves from the fear of being condemnatory or judgmental we can begin to speak the truth in love about abortion: that it can be harmful and destructive.

Releasing creativity in the church, creating alternative support structures

Filmmaker Julia Black, who filmed an entire abortion for a television documentary, said that she wished to challenge our 'lazy' thinking on the subject.[39] If we are serious about reducing the number of abortions in our society we need to create alternative support structures that offer women genuine choice. This may require effort and imagination, but it would certainly be better than pressurising women into something that many say afterwards they did not really want.

A creative example of an alternative support structure is provided by the "We Are Family" project, set up in 2005 by Alternatives Crisis Pregnancy Centre. The project acts as a catalyst to help single mothers and provides emotional and practical support, life skills and parenting skills to those with no wider family support structure. It is this sort of initiative that could come naturally to church communities once the silence around abortion is broken. There are many other initiatives that could be undertaken to encourage mothers to give birth or engage with the adoption process, but above all to encourage men to support women in their birth choices.

The assumption underpinning the promotion of abortion as the solution to unintended pregnancy is that it is something that many women will automatically want; that it will nearly always be the preferred '*choice*'.

What about women who would rather be pregnant? What do they want? Might large numbers of women actually want to experience pregnancy, to be pregnant and to give birth but feel unable to do so in a society that only offers abortion as a viable alternative? Could this be the reason for the high rate of pregnancy and subsequent abortion, and the high rate of repeat abortions? Perhaps creating new, imaginative support structures that encourage women to give birth and men to support this choice would empower women in their lives in a way that abortion does not. The message that can come across to some pregnant women is that they are viewed as useless and unvalued. As a society we are not prepared to offer them real choices.

Having an informed view is about engaging with the reality of abortion. It is about the reality that abortion leaves many women living with the nihilistic thought: *"I have participated in ending the life of my own child"*. It is about understanding the dynamics of contraception and the high risk of pregnancy in practice. It is about creating structures that enable women to be pregnant when they want to be and empower their choices. It is about giving women a real choice. It is about every pregnant woman feeling valued and protected.

Afterword

The importance of breaking the silence

In today's Christian culture it is entirely possible for someone to spend their whole life in a church and never hear the word abortion mentioned. By default, because the church has fallen silent, people assume that Christians agree with the (sometimes violent) protests that take place outside abortion clinics. Leaders seem unable to challenge this behaviour or provide an alternative. An unspoken cloud of condemnation and judgment thus hangs within the church. The silence has thus become a major barrier to the work of the gospel and evangelism. So many in our country have had their lives touched by abortion (either directly or through those close to them) that it must drive people away from the church and message of reconciliation found through the love of Jesus Christ. It is urgent that church leaders address the issue of abortion.

When designing the front cover of my book *Abortion – Breaking the silence in the church,* the graphic designer suggested the image of a woman whose mouth has been edited out, leaving her without a means of speaking. For me this image reflects the place that some women (and men) can find themselves after an abortion. The powerful culture of secrecy and shame around abortion can rob them of their voice, leaving them isolated and unable to speak about what they are experiencing. But for me there is another meaning to the image as well: it can also represent the position of the church. Until Christians can respond to the issue of abortion with clarity, compassion and confidence the church will be robbed of its voice and unable to respond to a number of other key issues facing our society in the field of medical ethics. It is essential that Christian scientists and medical professionals can become empowered to speak with confidence on ethical and life issues surrounding reproductive science, bio-technology and medicine, but until the silence is broken effectively around abortion, the church's ability to think and speak clearly on these matters will be compromised.

Appendix I

Rape and abortion

Questions around rape and abortion are highly charged and difficult to discuss without raising strong feelings. However, great though the temptation is to avoid the subject, I have noticed whenever speaking about our work in youth or church groups that this is the one question that is nearly always asked: people really want to know about and discuss this issue.

In our post abortion groups we have encountered women for whom this had been their experience, and we have ended up with a slightly different take on the issue. As with the wider picture of abortion, I think the best place to start thinking this through is to understand what is going on in our society.

A crime survey published in 2007[40] revealed the true extent of the horror of rape perpetrated against women in England and Wales. This authoritative and comprehensive study revealed that one in 20 women had been raped after the age of 16. One in 200 had been raped in the previous year. In terms of the population of England and Wales, 85,000 women are raped each year, equivalent to an average of 230 per day. This survey shows how the true extent of this crime is far greater than the officially reported figures of 11,000[41] for the same year (2007), or similar numbers of 14,000[42] for the most recent figures in 2010–11. Rape is a consistently underreported and hidden crime, and is widespread at many levels of our society.

Therefore, it is highly likely that a significant number of pregnancies and subsequent abortions take place as a result of rape every year.[43] Most people believe that in these circumstances the option of abortion should be available to women, and this completely understandable view has wide support in our culture. However, on our post-abortion recovery courses, a number of issues raised in connection with rape and abortion challenged my conventional thinking on the subject, leading me to suggest that they merit serious consideration. Counter-intuitively, some women who have been pregnant following a rape can come to feel that abortion is not necessarily the best option. This view has been expressed by some of the women who attended our course who had been subjected to rape (though not by all).

Perhaps this important point can start to be explored by relating the experience of two women who were rape survivors (but who had not become pregnant or experienced abortion) who attended one of our first groups. It was interesting for them to hear the stories of those who had been through abortion, and they both benefited greatly from being on the course. (They attended the course at the invitation of one of the leaders, who felt that they would benefit from our counselling expertise, given their lack of access to post-rape counselling at that time.)

At the end, one of the women said, "I had always assumed that had

I got pregnant as a result of my rape I would have had an abortion. But having heard these women's experiences I can now say that I would definitely not have an abortion, even as a result of being raped. It would be like being raped twice."

Why did she say that? What was it about what she had heard that made her change her mind?

A woman who has conceived as a result of being raped is being asked to make a hasty decision about an abortion under pressure and in dramatic circumstances, which have been forced upon her. She will be suffering from trauma and might find thinking about the present very difficult, let alone thinking about what might be best for her and what she might want for the future.

Although abortion appears to be a simple procedure, in this book we have considered the complications many women experience, which could add to the trauma of the rape. One of the course leaders reflected on her experience of counselling women who had been through rape and abortion, saying: "In choosing an abortion, you are not choosing whether to have the baby or not to have the baby. You are choosing between having the baby and having a traumatic experience. So on top of being raped it is choosing another traumatic experience."

In their book *Victims and Victors,* David Reardon, Julie Makimaa and Amy Sobie contrast a number of testimonies from women who have been in this position:

- Patricia, who was drugged and raped, became pregnant and had an abortion: "The effects of the abortion are much more far-reaching than the effects of the rape in my life" (Patricia Ryan).[44]

- Rebecca was raped by a friend and became pregnant. Following an abortion she said, "They say abortion is the easy way out, the best thing for everyone, but they are wrong. It has been over fifteen years and I still suffer" (Rebecca Morris).[45]

- Helene, who was raped during her first year at college, stated, "Abortion does not help or solve a problem, it only compounds and creates another trauma for the already grieving victim by taking away the one thing that can bring joy" (Helene Evans).[46]

It is commonly assumed that rape survivors who become pregnant would naturally want an abortion, but that is not necessarily always the case. Many may want to keep their child. To my knowledge there are no surveys available in Britain showing whether women who conceive as a result of rape wish to give birth to their children. However, one study in the US found just over 50% of rape survivors decided to continue with the pregnancy, with 32% deciding to keep their children, 6% releasing their child for adoption and 12% experiencing a miscarriage.[47]

Many women do not agree with abortion, and some victims of assault become introspective[48]; their sense of the value of life and respect for others is heightened, and to have an abortion would go against this. Others believe that if they can get through the pregnancy they will have conquered the rape: giving birth is proof that they are better than the rapist as, while he was selfish, the woman can be generous.

The following statement from Makimaa and Sobie's book is particularly compelling. They tell the story of Kathleen who was brutally raped and decided to place her child for adoption. During the pregnancy she changed her mind and decided to keep the child, "Once the baby continued to kick and move, I began to have different feelings towards the child. I began to realise that this little life inside of me was struggling too. Somehow my heart changed." (Kathleen DeZeeuw)[49]

Cindy was raped by a neighbour but decided to keep her child, "Through our children we begin to see more clearly what love and sacrifice are all about. To give life is to receive life in all its fullness." (Cindy Speltz)[50]

As explained earlier, our society tends to think that by making abortion available, a woman who becomes pregnant following rape has real choices. But is this true? Abortion may look compassionate, but what is the alternative? Where can a pregnant rape survivor go to be looked after while she decides what to do with her future? Where can she receive specialist counselling and support? Where is the place of security and anonymity where she could be loved and cared for during her pregnancy if she decides she would like to keep her child?

Where can a woman who comes from a culture in which discovery of a rape would result in her exclusion or persecution find shelter during her pregnancy, allowing her to rebuild her life on her own terms? Where is the adoption system adapted for the specific needs of women who have been raped and who wish to take time deciding on their future options, to see how they might feel about the child once it is born? Would it make a difference if it were a boy or a girl, for instance? There is pain in releasing a child for adoption, but from our experience on the post-abortion course, serious pain can also be caused by the guilt and trauma of an abortion.

Rape is about taking away a woman's choice, so I would suggest that the care and support that a woman is offered following a rape needs to be empowering. Although most people would understand that a woman in this position might choose to have an abortion, to assume automatically that this is in her best interests, or what she would always want is to inflict another wrong on someone on whom a great injustice has already been inflicted.

Many assume that a woman who has been raped might want an abortion because if she gave birth, she would be reminded of the rape every time she looked at the child, and that was certainly the reason why some of the rape survivors on our course chose abortion. But what people in general may not see is that a woman aborting a child conceived by rape is not just aborting the product of the rape: she is also aborting a deep part of her own motherhood, thus adding a further level of pain and potential trauma to the rape itself. Women wanting to keep their children can also come up against another hidden prejudice:

> "Because the actual experiences of pregnant sexual assault victims have not been widely heard, the social myth that abortion is the best, or even the only, option in cases of rape pregnancies is almost universally accepted. This universal myth creates its own set of problems for women. When a pregnant sexual assault victim balks at having an abortion, she will almost immediately faces queries of suspicion from family and friends. How can any woman have a rapist's child, they wonder? And then the suspicion mounts . . . maybe she lied. Maybe she was not really the victim of a 'legitimate' rape? And so the assumption that surely a real rape victim would want an abortion creates a new pressure on hurting women, in a time

> of intense crisis, to accept the recommendation of abortion, despite moral qualms and heightened sensitivity to victimization, to swallow their reservations and have the abortion if only to silence the rising doubts about their rape story."[51]

Of the 200 women that we have counselled, approximately ten had their abortions due to rape. Reflecting on their experiences, Nicky-Sue said this about rape and abortion:

> "Something that would be helpful here in considering whether abortion is right after a rape is to answer the question backwards, as it were. One of the women who came on the course who had had an abortion as the result of rape worked through the course alongside her group and found absolutely everything on the course to be entirely relevant to her. She dealt with exactly the same emotional issues and exactly the same thought processes.
>
> The decision making might have been a little different; there were, perhaps in her own mind, a few more arguments in favour of abortion for her, but the impact of the abortion was exactly the same. I think that in itself is an answer. She was as much a victim of the abortion as the rape. Of course, it is up to an individual woman to decide what she can stand, but a woman does not feel less guilt for having an abortion after being raped, she does not feel less grief following an abortion after she has been raped; it's exactly the same. After the powerful experience of being raped, the impact of abortion can be doubled in its effect really, because she sees it as something that was ultimately damaging to her. That has been helpful to me in my thinking and perhaps that is helpful for you too."

Some of the situations and stories we hear in the post-abortion healing group are simply terrible. Truly awful things can happen to women in our society through absolutely no fault of their own. But the heartbreak and distress of abortion is also more awful than is realised. There are no simple answers, no convenient solutions.

The challenge and opportunity is for the church and Christian organisations to fill the gap: to provide that place of shelter and love where women who have had a terrible wrong inflicted upon them can be protected and empowered to find the help and access to the services they need, at a time of their own choosing. They could be offered a place that will give them the space and time to decide whether or not they want to continue with the pregnancy, and possibly consider adoption for the baby, or to have an abortion. Whatever they choose, they will need help to rebuild their lives.

Appendix II

Disability, pre-natal screening and abortion

Central to the widespread acceptance of abortion in our culture is the situation where a disability has been identified during pregnancy, and a woman or a couple feel they could not cope with the situation. Approximately 2,000 abortions take place every year for this reason,[52] which represents around 1% of the total. This is a significant number and a very real and devastating dilemma for a great number of people.

As Christians, what should our response be as we consider this issue? How can we approach the subject in a way that might be of help to a woman or a couple who wish to enter into a screening programme (including foetal scanning), or to those who are entering a genetic counselling process prior to becoming pregnant? I believe that insights from the post-abortion counselling groups can bring a useful perspective.

Pre-natal screening during pregnancy

Before considering the issue of pre-natal screening and testing, it should be stressed that if, during a pregnancy, a medical practitioner advises a test that is aimed at protecting the health of mother and child, their advice should be taken.

Access to genetic information has increased enormously in the past few years. Pre-natal testing and screening procedures are becoming ever more accurate and sophisticated. In advanced industrial countries, pre-natal testing for detecting foetal abnormalities has become routine. In Britain at present two ultrasound scans are offered to all women between 11 and 13 weeks and between 18 and 21 weeks. The aim of these scans is to date the pregnancy, diagnose multiple pregnancies, confirm placental location, and to identify foetal anomalies. Therefore it is highly likely that a pregnant woman in Britain will be offered an array of different screening options, from scans and blood tests to more invasive procedures such as amniocentesis or Chorionic Villus Sampling (CVS) if further tests are being recommended.

This is an issue, therefore, that every woman or couple needs to think about carefully when a pregnancy has begun, because virtually every pregnant woman in the UK will be offered some form of pre-natal screening, including a pre-natal scan.

One might assume that this is a process designed to provide reassurance to a pregnant mother or couple. However, I would suggest that the medical reality is that screening tests are offered in order to make abortion available as an option should an abnormality be detected.

While in a very small number of cases it might be possible to intervene medically if a problem were discovered, for the overwhelming majority of cases where an abnormality is detected, a termination of the pregnancy would be offered. It is important to understand that although pre-natal scanning can produce wonderful images of life growing in the womb – images that perhaps reassure a pregnant mother and help her bond with her baby – those undertaking the scanning process are often looking for abnormalities. It could be said that by agreeing to a scan, one is *de facto* entering into a screening process.

By the time most abnormalities are detected, a pregnancy will probably be in the second or third trimester (more than fourteen weeks), which is late for an abortion, and so a medical professional would almost certainly recommend that if a decision for abortion is to be made, it should be made as soon as possible, perhaps even the same day as the diagnosis.

The pressure to reach a hasty decision can turn what is a stressful situation into one of panic. Therefore, it would be helpful for anyone embarking on pre-natal testing (including a foetal scan) to think through its possible implications, and to discuss the matter of abortion with a partner in advance of any situation where it might become a possibility.

Being presented with the devastating news that a wanted child will have a disability must turn a woman or couple's world upside down in an instant and leave them fearful for the future. The prospect of bringing a child into the world where the odds are stacked against them might just seem too difficult to bear, and the responsibility of making such a decision could seem almost more painful than choosing abortion. It is easy to see how an abortion could appear to be the kindest thing for all concerned, both in the interests of parents and the child, and possibly also for any other children. It can be hard enough to raise able-bodied children and the world can seem an unforgiving place. But is abortion really in the best interests of those concerned?

As discussed at length in earlier chapters, our perspective from the post-abortion counselling course is that abortion does not wind back the clock and there can be unexpected consequences to an abortion. Where a disability has been discovered several weeks into a pregnancy, there could be an added level of complication because a mother has had time to bond with her baby at a deeper level and the child has become precious and wanted.

The pressure to have an abortion might be perceived as something that is being forced upon her by outside circumstances rather than originating from within, leading to a powerful feeling of coercion and loss of control, even though it is actually the woman (or the couple) who makes the decision.

At the heart of a diagnosis of abnormality or disability lies a quite understandable fear: fear of the future and what a disability might mean. My advice to anyone in this position would be to take time and not to make an abortion decision in haste. Facing our fears can sometimes help dispel them. There are many specialised support groups that can offer help and advice, and ultimately for parents who felt they could not cope there might be the alternative of adoption (although in practice this is rarely considered in this situation).

As Christians we believe, and may have heard preached, that where a disability has been diagnosed during pregnancy, the foetus is still a human being and therefore has a right to life. However, we all have our limitations and do not know how we may respond to such a challenge. Legalistic language is not helpful to a woman where an abnormality has been diagnosed, and people in this situation need encouragement to take life one step at a time and to receive the help and support they might need. They could be invited to look at the possibility of adoption (depending on what has been diagnosed) in the event that they could not cope, thus being offered a genuine choice in this situation, which might help to lift the burden of responsibility and encourage parents to continue with the pregnancy.

Women especially in this situation need unconditional love, even if there is talk of an abortion, and the support of our churches in offering more practical support and ministries for those with physical and mental disabilities. My godmother, Mary Straw, runs a house church in Montreal (the Julia Kraft Centre) for those with severe mental disabilities. She struggles to form links and to receive support from local churches because her ministry just does not fit in with traditional structures. Perhaps this is a gap in our model of doing church. If we are to be serious about challenging the widespread cultural acceptance of abortion in the case of disability, perhaps we are the ones who should be doing the rethinking in terms of engaging with those who have different needs.

Genetic counselling prior to becoming pregnant

Genetic counselling can be helpful for people who are concerned about a specific genetic disease. It normally involves a short-term educational process for individuals and families at risk of a genetic disease, those who have a family history of a genetic disease, or those who are considering genetic testing. Genetic counsellors are trained healthcare professionals with experience in medical genetics, ethics, healthcare and counselling. They are trained to help families understand genetic disorders and provide information and support to those families.

There are a variety of circumstances that may lead someone to seek advice from a genetic counsellor. For those at risk of having a baby with a disorder, genetic counselling can help:

- Assess the risk of genetic disorders by researching their family history for any genetic diseases;
- Weigh the medical and ethical issues of genetic testing;
- Decide if they should undergo carrier testing before pregnancy;
- Decide if they should become pregnant;
- Decide if they should have pre-natal testing;
- Interpret the results of the testing;
- Explain possible treatments or preventative measures for genetic diseases.

While genetic counselling can be a process that might dispel fear and help assess risk, it is important for individuals, especially Christians, to work out their views on abortion prior to entering into the genetic counselling process, and to make it clear to a counsellor if abortion is not an option for them.

It is especially important to ask what pre-natal tests might be offered during a pregnancy and if any treatments would be available if a condition were present. Some diagnostic tests present a risk of miscarriage (for example amniocentesis or Chorionic Villus Sampling (CVS)), and although these tests might offer reassurance during pregnancy, I have had conversations with distraught parents who have miscarried following such tests. If abortion is off the list of options it might be best to question the value of invasive testing once a pregnancy has begun.

Summary

It may be hard for some of us to think of life with a disability as desirable, and on one television programme debating the subject of euthanasia I heard a severely disabled person stating that they wished they had never been born. But I do not believe that this is the case for the overwhelming majority of people born with disabilities, many of whom live full and fascinating lives. While it is tempting in Christian circles to point to such giants as Nick Vujicic, who was born without arms or legs and preaches to millions of people around the world, the overwhelming majority of people with disabilities will lead ordinary, but wholly worthwhile and fulfilling lives. Each and every one of us remains precious in God's eyes from conception to death.

Acknowledgements

So many wonderful women have helped organise and lead the Post-Abortion Healing Course at Holy Trinity Brompton since we started in 1993, that it would be difficult for me to produce a complete list going back 20 years. But it is with the women of the counselling teams that my chief thanks must lie, as without their selfless devotion this book would not have been possible. Thank you so much for the countless hours that you spent bringing healing and peace to so many women and men. Perhaps I could mention by name the team leaders: Nicky-Sue Leonard, Caryn Dixon, Terese Williamson and now Jo Chambers.

The consistent support of (now Bishop) Sandy Millar, followed by Nicky Gumbel, Bob Read and Nicky and Sila Lee, has been a key factor in helping to develop the ministry. My thanks in particular to Jenny Baines who did an excellent job of initially editing the book, and to Julia Evans who really helped to shape the project.

Lastly there is one person who deserves particular mention: my dear wife Francesca, who has supported steadfastly in this ministry for 20 years. Thank you for your steady encouragement and support – thank you from the bottom of my heart.

Notes

[1] Department of Health, 2011. *Abortion Statistics England and Wales: 2010.* London: Department of Health, p.17, Table 4b. See also Appendix VII.

[2] Royal College of Obstetricians and Gynaecologists, 2004. *The Care of Women Requesting Induced Abortion, 2004.* London: Royal College of Obstetricians and Gynaecologists, p.1.

[3] Department of Health, 2011. *Abortion Statistics England and Wales: 2010.* London: Department of Health, p.7. [These figures broadly reflect the general population of the United Kingdom with some slight exceptions, especially among the repeat abortion figures (Table A), which show the overrepresentation of some non-white ethnic groups.]

[4] Department of Health, 2011. *Abortion Statistics England and Wales: 2010.* London: Department of Health, p.15, Table 3a.

[5] Department of Health, 2011. *Abortion Statistics England and Wales: 2010.* London: Department of Health, p.8, paragraph 2.9. [In 2010, 831 abortions were performed under Ground E (congenital deformity) out of a total of 189,574, or 0.43%.]

[6] Bury, L. and Ngo, T., 2009. *"The Condom Broke!" Why do Women in the UK Have Unintended Pregnancies?* London: Marie Stopes International, p.20. [At the time of the unintended pregnancy, 62% of women reported using a contraceptive method.]

[7] Schünmann, C. and Glasier, A., 2006. *Measuring Pregnancy Intention and its Relationship with Contraception Use Among Women Undergoing Therapeutic Abortion.* Association of Reproductive Health Professionals: Contraception Journal, volume 73, issue 5, pp.520–524. [In a study of 316 women in

Scotland, 16% were not using contraception, while 44% were using it inconsistently or incorrectly.]

[8] Bury, L. and Ngo, T., 2009. *"The Condom Broke!" Why do Women in the UK Have Unintended Pregnancies?* London: Marie Stopes International, p.8. [Most women who report for abortion counselling say they had no desire to get pregnant, and almost all have information about and access to a variety of contraceptive methods.]

[9] Porter, M., 2009. It's Time to Think Again About Your Choice of Contraception.

The Times, 26 January. See also: Trussell, J., 2007. Contraceptive Efficacy. In: Hatcher, R.A. et al eds., 2007. *Contraceptive Technology: Nineteenth Revised Edition.* New York, NY: Ardent Media. See also NHS Clinical Knowledge Summaries, 2012. *Contraception – Background information: How effective are the various contraceptive methods?* [online] Available at: http://www.cks.nhs.uk/contraception_background_information/effectiveness_of_contraception [Accessed 13 April 2012.]

[10] NHS Choices, 2010. *How effective is contraception at preventing pregnancy?* [online] Available at: <http://www.nhs.uk/chq/Pages/825.aspx?CategoryID=117&SubCategoryID=114> [Accessed 04 November 2011.] [Success rate for the combined pill is in excess of 99% "if taken correctly" and 98% for condom use "if used correctly".]

[11] Lewis, C.S., 1977. *The Screwtape Letters: Letters from a Senior to a Junior Devil.* Glasgow: William Collins and Sons, Ltd., p.44.

[12] Bury, L. and Ngo, T., 2009. *"The Condom Broke!" Why do Women in the UK Have Unintended Pregnancies?* London: Marie Stopes International.

[13] Bristow, J., 2008–09. *Abortion Review Special Edition* 2. London: BPAS.

[14] Moran, C., 2007. Abortion: Why it's the Ultimate Motherly Act. *The Times*, 13 April, 2007.

[15] Department of Health, 2011. *Abortion Statistics England and Wales: 2010*, p.17. London: Department of Health.

[16] Wood, G., 2011. Cracknell and Moore Show that Emotion is a Masculine Issue. *The Daily Telegraph*, 2 June.

[17] Lewis, C.S., 1952. *Mere Christianity* Book 3, Chapter 7. Oxford: Harper Collins.

[18] ten Boom, C. 1971. *The Hiding Place*. London. Hodder & Stoughton.

[19] See: Rue, V., 1996. *The Effects of Abortion on Men*. Ethics and Medicine 21 (4): 3–4; Condon, G., and Hazard, D., 2001. *Fatherhood Aborted*. Carol Stream: Tyndale House; and Coyle, C., 1999. *Men and Abortion: A Path to Healing*. Fort Collins: Life Cycle Books; and Jones, K. and Cochrane, L., 1996. *Healing a Father's Heart: a Post-Abortion Bible Study for Men*. Ada, Michigan: Baker Books.

[20] Reardon, D., 1987. *Aborted Women Silent No More*. Chicago: Loyola University Press. Foreword by Mann, N., pp.x–xii.

[21] Bristow, J., 2008–09. Why do people get pregnant (when they don't want to be?). *Abortion Review*. London: BPAS.

[22] Greer, G., 2000. *The Whole Woman*. London: Anchor Books, p.109.

[23] Ibid., p.xi.

[24] Office for National Statistics, 2011. *Marriage, Divorce and Adoption Statistics 2010*. London: Office for National Statistics.

[25] Utting, D. and Bewley, S., 2011. Family Planning and Age-Related risk. *The Obstetrician & Gynaecologist 2011, 13: 35–41.*

[26] Office for National Statistics, 2010. *Abortion Statistics, England and Wales 2010*. London: Office for National Statistics. [In 2010, 139,510 women aged 29 or under had an abortion of a total 189,574.]

[27] Utting, D. and Bewley, S., 2011. Family Planning and Age-Related Risk. *The Obstetrician & Gynaecologist, 2011, 13: 35–41.* [At the age of 25, just 5% of women take longer than a year to conceive and this rises to 30% in women aged 35.]

[28] Fertilisation and Embryology Authority, 2011. *Fertility Treatment in 2010, Trends and Figures*. London: Human Fertilisation and Embryology Authority. [The overall success rate for IVF in the UK is approximately 34%.]

[29] Moran, C., 2011. *How to Be a Woman*. London: Ebury Press, p.284.

[30] Reardon, D., 1996. *Making Abortion Rare*. Springfield: Acorn Books, p.152.

[31] Bury, L. and Ngo, T., 2009. *"The Condom Broke!" Why do Women in the UK*

Have Unintended Pregnancies? London: Marie Stopes International, p.7. ["Reducing the number of unintended pregnancies in the UK is a desirable and achievable goal."]

[32] Joyce, A., 2000. *"The Only Moral Abortion is My Abortion". When the Anti-Choice Choose.* [online] Available at: <http://mypage.direct.ca/w/writer/anti-tales.html>. [Accessed 5 November 2011.]

[33] Office for National Statistics, 2011. *Conceptions in England and Wales 2009.* London: Office for National Statistics.

[34] Lader, D., 2009. *Opinions Survey Report No. 41: Contraception and Sexual Health, 2008–09.* London: Office for National Statistics.

[35] Bury, L. and Ngo, T., 2009. *"The Condom Broke!" Why do Women in the UK Have Unintended Pregnancies?* London: Marie Stopes International.

[36] Trussell, J., 2008. Why Contraception Fails. In: *BPAS, Abortion Review Special Edition 2, Winter 2008–09.* London: BPAS.

[37] Reason, J., 1990. *Human Error*. Cambridge: Cambridge University Press.

[38] King, M.L., 1963. *Letter from Birmingham Jail (April 1963)* cited in Martin Luther King Day Quotes. [online] Gainesville: University of Florida (Published 1997). Available at <http:// grove.ufl.edu/~leo/mlk.html>. [Accessed 10 September 2007.]

[39] Black, J., 2004. My Abortion and My Baby, *The Guardian* [online] Available at: <http://www.guardian.co.uk/media/2004/apr/04/channel4.medicineandhealth> [Accessed 18 September 2011.]

[40] Povey, D., et al., 2008. *Statistical Bulletin: Homicides, Firearms Offences and Intimate Violence 2006–7 Third Edition.* London: Home Office.

[41] Home Office, 2008. *Statistical Bulletin: Crime in England and Wales 2007–08.* London: Home Office. [The bulletin records 11,648 offences of rape in England and Wales during this period.]

[42] Home Office, 2010. *Statistical Bulletin: Crime in England and Wales 2010–11.* UK: Home Office. [The bulletin records 14,624 offences of rape in England and Wales during this period.]

[43] One large-scale study of in the US estimated a national rape-related pregnancy rate of 5% amongst victims aged 12–45. Of these 32% opted to keep

their child, 50% underwent abortion, 6% placed the child for adoption and 12% had miscarriages. Similar figures applied to UK rates would mean 1–2% of all UK abortions were due to rape. See: Holmes M,. Resnick H,. Kilpatrick D,. Best C,.1996: Rape-related pregnancy: estimates and descriptive characteristics from a national sample of women. Charleston USA. Medical University of South Carolina, 1996 Aug; 175(2):320–4.

[44] Reardon, D., Makimaa, J., and Sobie, A., 2010. *Victims and Victors.* Springfield: Acorn Books, p.52.

[45] Ibid., p.63.

[46] Ibid,. p.67.

[47] Holmes M,. Resnick H,. Kilpatrick D,. Best C,. 1996: Rape-related pregnancy: estimates and descriptive characteristics from a national sample of women. Charleston USA. Medical University of South Carolina, 1996 Aug; 175(2):320–4.

[48] Ibid., p.14.

[49] Ibid., p.74.

[50] Ibid., p.95.

[51] Schroeder, D, 2012: My Rape Pregnancy and My Furor Over Social Myths. Washington: Ad Hoc Committee of Women Pregnant By Sexual Assault (WPSA).

[52] Department of Health, 2011. *Abortion Statistics England and Wales: 2010.* London: Department of Health, Table 9. [Congenital malformations were reported as the principal medical condition in nearly half (48%; 1,094) of the 2,290 cases undertaken under Ground E of the Abortion Act. The most commonly reported malformations were of the nervous system (23% of all Ground E cases; 522) and the musculoskeletal system (8%; 181). Chromosomal abnormalities were reported as the principal medical condition for just over a third (36%; 831) of Ground E cases. Down's syndrome was the most commonly reported chromosomal abnormality (21% of all Ground E cases; 482).]

The Post-Abortion Healing Course at Holy Trinity Brompton, London

This course is for women who have been through abortion(s). It is designed for Christians who wish to receive healing and restoration in this area. The course offers a safe place for women to share experiences in a small group setting and to work through the different emotions and consequences following the abortion decision. Confidentiality is always respected.

The course is run over eight sessions, including a full Saturday. Each evening begins with a meal, followed by an interactive talk, discussion/sharing and prayer.

Registration is via email or phone, or by post.
You can register with your first name only, if you prefer.

What one woman said about the course:
'I felt very safe and had an opportunity for openness and truth about an issue that was very difficult. Here I felt safe enough to revisit my abortion in an environment that was equipped to handle the consequences effectively and led by individuals who were informed and some of whom had been in a similar position.'

For details of the next course see:
www.htb.org.uk/post-abortion-healing or contact:
courses@htb.org.uk or **020 7052 0323** for further information.

If you would like information on how to set up and lead a post abortion discussion group in your church please contact:
info@leanpress.co.uk